the girl in the treehouse

"*The Girl in the Treehouse* will rip your heart open as you walk through the thorns of Jennifer's childhood, then sew it back together with threads of forgiveness and love. A powerful literary journey flowing with wit, humor, heartache, and inspiration."

—Pamela Cangioli, *Literary reviewer*

"Author Jennifer Asbenson is a brave women. This book is amazing, and I recommend to anyone that is suffering from PTSD. After everything she went through, here she stands—a true warrior."

—Stacey Mullens, *Psychiatric RN*

"I stayed up all night reading this book. Amazing! I wanted to hug the author through it all. Such evil, but Jennifer endured with bright resilience. I felt like she was staring into my soul with love and hope."

—Jan Sportswood-Sumner, *Bipolar*

"Inspirational and emotive storytelling at its finest! *The Girl in the Treehouse* is a raw, poignant, and powerful read. Jennifer's story bears testimony to the strength, courage, and determination of the human spirit. Though heartbreaking at times, it acts as a reminder that it is possible to overcome trauma and embrace the warrior within."

—Rebecca Millar, *Bestselling mental health author*

"Gripping and emotional, and leaves you wanting to keep reading more and more. Heartbreaking and amazing. A must read."

—Charles Erwin, *PTSD survivor*

The Girl in the Treehouse
Jennifer Asbenson

the girl in the treehouse

JENNIFER ASBENSON

First Edition
Softcover ISBN: 978-1727802245

Book Consultant and Designer: Patricia Bacall

Editor: Jennifer McGrath

Proofreader: Proofed to Perfection

Printed in the United States of America on acid-free paper.

Follow us on social media

Facebook Discussion Group: The Girl in the Treehouse Group

Twitter: @jenasbenson

Instagram: jenniferasbenson

www.thegirlinthetreehousebook.com

Dedication

This book is dedicated to the eight angels in heaven
whom I've never met but know very well.

Foreword

The Girl in the Treehouse will immerse you in the author's world of beauty and heartache, innocence and doubt, despair and unshakable hope, then take you on a journey from her wounded childhood to her job with special children, from her traumatic escape from a serial killer to her years of struggle toward healing.

Jennifer Asbenson's book is raw, honest, and heart-wrenching. She has opened a portal to a deep and powerful place where only the courageous dare enter—a revelation not only of one's life, but of one's soul.

The Girl in the Treehouse isn't a self-help book that will tell you what you should and should not do. It isn't for those who expect safety and perfection. No, it will not take you there. Instead, it will take you to where childhood dreams are brutally shattered and cast away. It will take you to where trust is repaid by the utmost form of betrayal. It will take you to that very point where you start to question just how much pain the human heart can possibly bear.

But such darkness is interspersed with light. That's what really tears your heart apart. Throughout everything Jennifer has suffered, she has almost always found a way to see the good things that still remain. We see how art, imagination, and a sense of humor helped her find an escape where there seemed to be none. We see how, despite everything she suffered, she still found the strength to forgive, to hope, and to love.

Jennifer tells her story with such frankness and openness of heart that she leaves herself vulnerable to all of us who may try to judge her actions or past decisions. We can examine her life, but we can only do so if we also judge and examine our own.

What prompted people to act the way they did? What were the consequences of those actions? When we really look through the eyes of the author, we see not only the impact of her life and her decisions on others, but we also see how each person from her childhood up to the present has helped shape her own life.

It is dangerous to see everything in black and white, void of the many shades and colors in between. But Jennifer has succeeded at painting a story of her own life on a canvas that shows far more than what we can initially see. Life is like that. Life is not made up of just one layer of story, but layers upon layers of truth interwoven together in a tapestry that we can only appreciate when seen as a whole.

Jennifer's story has not yet ended, but she has allowed us to look deep within, painfully deep into all its lights and shadows. She has welcomed us into her "treehouse," into that place where she can be broken and healed, where she can bleed and laugh, and start over again.

In the end, Jennifer never asks to be seen as the perfect role model. By showing us herself through a lens of complete honesty, she asks to be seen as perfectly imperfect. Her task has always been to be the voice of those who cannot speak for themselves—to be a storyteller. And this she has done very well in *The Girl in the Treehouse*.

—Jocelyn Soriano,
  Poet, Blogger, Novelist, and Author of *Mend My Broken Heart*

A Few Words from the Author

Over the years, I have received numerous letters through social media, postal mail, and other outlets. Many people have referred to me as a warrior in these letters. The term is gladly accepted. As a warrior, I promise to encourage you and to inspire you to follow your dreams. I also promise to remind you that you, too, are a warrior.

My Dear Warriors,

It gives me great pleasure to know you're willing to fight for your dreams, regardless of the disappointments and scars that you've had to live with. I'm glad you've come to seek out the things that really matter in life. So, despite the distractions and the misinformation bombarding you, you are still able to hold your head high and maintain your focus and perspective.

I can imagine the many twists and turns that have happened to you and how you've made it through each one of them, notching various badges of honor on your way through. It thrills me to announce that whatever your brilliant mind can imagine can one day be your reality.

Our ability to maintain an imaginative frame of mind amid the circumstances surrounding us is the most powerful weapon we have to fight against the harmful behavior of negative and manipulative people around us. If you can remove yourself from these people, please do so. If you are trapped, you must love yourself enough to free your mind from the situation.

You have the power to be your own storyteller; don't let anyone tell your story for you. You are not obliged to give in to people who try to impose their own interpretation of things on you. You must be strong, forgive, and forge ahead. Do not allow others to get behind the wheel of your life.

Think of where you would have been today if you had allowed many of the people in the past—who wanted to walk all over you and run your life—to have their way. But for the most part, you are here today because of the choices you've willfully made. That highlights how crucial your will has been to your journey on this mortal planet.

When there's a will, there's a weapon, and your will is the magic wand that can turn your dreams into reality. You hold the magic.

That assertion is applicable to any circumstance in which you might find yourself, including sexual abuse, child abuse, mental illness, and even life-threatening situations. So, even when your mental faculties aren't functioning the way they should, you still have all the internal resources needed to turn things around.

History is replete with countless people who overcame huge odds against them and achieved things that others thought were impossible. Their remarkable turnaround was mostly due to their resolution and perseverance to wrestle the odds to the ground. You, too, can confront your circumstances with a similar resolve, in order to bolster your chances of coming out on top.

The day you find the faith I have in you, within yourself, is the day you will conquer the world.

Acknowledgments

To Gregg, I thank you for your unyielding faith in me and your generous and relentless support.

I wish to thank all the people who joined forces with me to turn my abstract book idea into a full-fledged book. I'm sending the warmest regards to my brilliant editor, Jennifer McGrath, my phenomenal book consultant and designer, Patricia Bacall, and my diligent proofreader, Pamela Cangioli, all of whom helped me refine and polish my work. Each of you provided my work with inputs from the "sixth sense," which I'm yet to possess. You are the turners of dreams into realities.

I also wish to give special thanks to my friends and family who have encouraged my book to the moon and back. You've helped fuel the fire in my bones that inspired me to write every single page of this book. I am grateful that you have all invested tremendous amounts of positive energy and empowering vibes into my life.

And to you, my lion-hearted warrior, I want you to know that I can feel your energy right here inside my soul, even if you are light-years away from my location. All I can see are blessings, blessings, and more blessings surrounding you. I see the universe dealing you a favorable hand as you go up against the odds. And for what it's worth, I completely and totally know that you have the strength to overcome the forces you think might be working against your best interests right now. It only takes one person's belief to change things around, and I have faith in you. Be the warrior you were destined to be. If I did it, you can too.

Prologue

My name is Jennifer Asbenson. I am forty-three years old, and I live in a treehouse.

My life has been a roller-coaster ride. This treehouse feels like a safe place to be completely vulnerable, so let me start by telling you something that shocks most people. When I was nineteen, I escaped from a serial killer who murdered eight women. I am the only one who got away. But the kidnapping and escape are just a small part of my life.

I grew up in an abusive household with no electricity or water. As a child, I was given responsibility for my handicapped brother. I kept him on a rope so that he couldn't get away. I was shy, innocent, and naive. I have been through a great deal in life and survived most of it with the help of God, humor, and my imagination. It has been a tough road, but out of everything I've been through, loving myself was the most difficult feat.

I am in the treehouse because one night, not too long ago, my heart was broken by the man in the house. I retreated to the guest room with a full bottle of wine, my cell phone, my laptop, and my earphones. Tears flowed fast and hard until I hyperventilated. Kenny Rogers sang to me while I watched Christmas cartoons on mute.

The experience of the entire situation was a beautiful mess. I cried, I laughed, I drank wine, and, screw it—I'll be honest—I smoked some pot as well. That same night and half-a-bottle of wine later, I decided I would write a book and finally tell my story. For some reason, I am most creative when I am enveloped by emotional turmoil. I decided I couldn't live in the house anymore and determined the treehouse in the backyard would be sufficient.

The next morning, I woke with swollen eyes and an empty wine bottle beside me. I also had a horrific headache. Before I got out of bed, the man in the house knocked on my barricaded door.

He gently pried the door open and asked, "Would you like a cup of coffee?"

"Yes, of course." I was grateful for his kindness.

"I am going to move into the treehouse and write a book," I said. Even with a throbbing head and a tear-streaked face, my words were spoken with resolution and confidence.

I don't think he took me seriously.

I NOW LIVE IN THE treehouse in his backyard, about twenty feet away from the house.

Now, I must tell you that the man in the house is not a bad person at all. There are just some things in a relationship I no longer tolerate. I am codependent with a tendency toward relationship addiction. And I have had my share of unhealthy relationships. But I am not disabled; I chose to end this cycle by not accepting any form of disrespect. I made a conscious decision some years ago to end relationships that cause me pain in any way, big or small, because they are unhealthy and not spiritually satisfying. It is very hard to leave these relationships. Some unhealthy relationships in my past took acts of God to end.

I don't know what will become of the man in the house and me. All I do know is that I feel safest by myself. And maybe, if I stay in this treehouse long enough, I'll find and fall in love with the person who has always helped me through turbulent times—myself.

CHAPTER ONE

Wind and Wine

*L*ast night I peed into a bucket. It wasn't all that strange. The alternative to the bucket had been to climb down a cold, wobbly ladder, in the dark, and tiptoe through wet grass. The grass was an absolute minefield of dog poop, concealed by the night, and still grotesquely wet. As bad as the bucket may have seemed at the outset, I'll bet it sounds pretty good now. It did to me. In fact, I considered the bucket to be a luxury.

The perfect choice was a medium-sized, metal bucket with the words *Huge Balls* written on the side. At our last Christmas party, I had filled the bucket with fake snowballs. We had a snowball fight that I will never forget. But don't worry; I will not use it again at future parties for any reason, unless somebody needs to urinate and the bathrooms are all occupied.

I'm no stranger to life off the grid. For most of my childhood, my dad worked hard to build us a home in the desert. It was a geodesic house—an igloo-shaped structure made from wood—that took him years to develop. Life was primitive. For the most part, I grew up with no electricity or reliable water sources.

We had a double-seater outhouse. Why my dad made it with two seats, I cannot imagine. Not once did two people go in together and do their business as they chatted away about their day, and I'm almost certain no one would ever want to. The outhouse was my last resort for typical restroom use. As a child, I would usually go into the desert and find a private spot behind a bush instead. Unless the day was hot, then I was afraid a hidden snake might bite my bottom. To this day, I disapprove of outhouses. Intense toilet phobia is brought on by the thought that some animal would try to climb up on me after I squat.

Without electricity, there was no heater to keep us warm, no air conditioner to keep us cool, no TV to watch, and no washer and dryer to keep our clothes clean. We weren't left with much. Jackets and blankets were great, if they were clean. Pillows disappeared more than teeth—we never went to the dentist or brushed our teeth, so we lost a lot of them.

We also had no water. No water meant no showers, no baths, no clean clothes, not much of anything that required the liquid commodity.

We lived out in the middle of nowhere. In school, I felt like an outcast. I spoke very little in order to avoid attention from others. When I had something to say, I would stifle myself with a quick reminder of my reality—that I had nothing worth saying.

If I did speak, it would be to dream: "Imagine if …" or "Pretend that …" I always imagined and pretended. In a way, this was how I dealt with my living situation. And eventually, I began to see things that were not there. My eyes would turn shacks into castles. Everything had potential and beauty. Although I wore the same dress to school every day, I pretended to be wealthy. I kept my imaginary status to myself at school; the other kids would have seen through the make-believe anyway.

We went a few weeks without water until the day we discovered a waterspout on the back of a local convenience store. We would haul buckets and jugs, sneak behind the store, and fill them. If I ever saw anyone walk near the store, I would hide. I was too embarrassed to be seen, one of several nightmare situations for me during my childhood. But at least we had water.

Surely, after I had a bath I'd be instantly popular, one of the cool kids. Life would be golden. Sadly, this never came true.

Washing your body and hair outside in cold weather isn't much fun, so I would pretend in this situation too. I would put my mind anywhere else to trick it. I would bathe maybe once a month, but I was never referred to as smelly. Well, I never personally referred to myself as smelly!

One day, my mom came home excited; she had found a random waterspout on the side of a road. We had a light blue, flatbed truck with wooden rails. My dad took off the rails and put a large, square tank on the back. My mom would use pliers and a hose to fill the tank. We always needed tools to turn the spigot on because someone removed the knob for some reason, probably to stop people from doing what we did.

One of my worst fears manifested when I was in middle school. My mom decided to fill the truck with water after school while she waited to pick me up at the bus stop. The spout was at the bus stop, in full view of all the kids on my bus. If I wanted a ride from my mom the two miles back home, I had to get off at that bus stop. I was sure the kids would say, "Hey, Jennifer, your mom's stealing water again." I was so embarrassed that I would purposely skip my bus stop, get off at the next stop, and walk the four or five blocks back to where my mom was stealing water.

My dad was brilliant at invention and construction. He constructed a shower near our half-built house and placed a fifty-gallon drum on top of the structure, with a spout that released the water. My dad parked the truck up the hill on what we called the top pad—a flat, cleared space, higher on the mountain, above our house. A long hose snaked from the water tank downhill to the drum and—*bam!* We had an instant shower. It was like winning a jackpot.

Nothing motivates speed in the shower better than cold water. The frigid drops forced me to dance, and my imagination helped me through it. My coping method started as the simple image of a shower at the beach. As the images grew more elaborate, I would close my eyes, sing in a high-pitched voice, and imagine the dolphins, the heat of the sun, and the rhythmic ocean waves. The scene soon developed into my own special world. The ice-cold water had diamonds in it, too tiny to see. It was a cleansing reserved for the super-rich, the people like me. The rejuvenating effects of the diamonds meant that the colder you got, the more beautiful you would become. From my earlier jumping and shaking to stay warm, a sacred dance evolved. I moved my feet rapidly, without lifting my toes off the ground, and flapped my hands up and down, side to side, with my elbows fixed to my hips. This was a weekly, sometimes bi-weekly, routine that would last through my teen years.

We had animals out there in the desert, too: a goat named, Dolly, and her baby, Alphie. I witnessed his birth. The experience was beautiful but bloody. He was so cute, and his ears were so soft. Sometimes he slept with me. The milk we drank came from Dolly. To milk her, we tied her to a tree so she could not run. I would put cereal in whatever I could find that resembled a bowl and squirt Dolly's milk from her goat boobies straight into the bowl. I would pretend to be rich. So rich, in fact, I drank hot goat milk with my Cheerios. There was severe imagination going on here, as the actual taste took some stomaching. My vomit reflex was always on high alert during Cheerios time.

I'm about to pour a glass of red wine and tell you all about my little treehouse. In this treehouse of mine, I recall the past like it was yesterday. I know how to live like this, primitively, but I didn't ever imagine I'd be living in a treehouse when I was forty-three. Life can throw the unexpected at you, like a new adventure—an adventure where nothing is missing, except for maybe a goat or two.

This night is a fantastic night in my treehouse. My heater is aglow, and the temperature is just perfect. The evening is unique because it is windy outside. It is my first stormy night in the tree. I'm sure I will experience and survive all the weather conditions life will throw at me except snow and tornadoes, but we don't get those here. The thought of an earthquake did run through my mind as well. Mother Nature is more intriguing than scary to me, and if an earthquake did happen, my ten belongings here would be easily replaced, apart from maybe the wine.

The Lumineers entertain in the background while I sip my wine—Francis Coppola Diamond Collection Cabernet, to be precise. Incense burns every night. Tonight, it is Nag Champa. I am loyal to Nag

Champa. Some say incense has spiritual uses, such as to sanctify or purify an area. I believe it's working. I feel as pure as the first driven snow. I also burn white sage. For hundreds of years, white sage has been considered a sacred, cleansing, purifying, and protective plant. I feel very protected.

My treehouse is covered with Moroccan tapestries that give off a musty odor, as if a wet dog slept on them for years. More likely than that, I simply inhaled the scent of cheap dye. The burn of white sage and incense helps, maybe even complements the smell in a way. Some of the tapestry's colors are oddly saturated by the glow of my Christmas lights. Instead of the traditional red, green, or rainbow string of lights, mine is comprised of deep purple and blue bulbs. The cool glow has a slight inconsistency that soothes, as every fifth and sixth light flickers, while the rest burn continuously. Either they were designed this way by some hippie-treehouse-light-effect genius, or my staple gun missed its mark, crimped the wire, and created a short that triggered this welcomed side effect that aims to mesmerize.

Under the tapestry is plastic, hidden completely. When insulating your treehouse, you can choose from a variety of materials. I favored plastic. It works splendidly. The floor is layered with ugly rugs underneath and a large, beautiful carpet on top. It is all about layers when living off the grid.

One thing I cannot regulate is the weather. It has become a true adventure now. As I describe my luxuriously humble surroundings to you, the treehouse rocks in the wind and the branches wildly hit the sheet-metal roof. I hear sirens wail and dogs bark. Pandora plays Ray LaMontagne's "Trouble," as if the universe is saying, "Time to go home, crazy lady." Mother Nature doesn't know me as well as she thinks.

Not speaking is a surreal experience. I haven't spoken a single word in what feels like an eternity—for three hours, according to my phone. I feel like a monk in monastic silence—a spiritual practice in various religious traditions, where monks or other holy people are quiet for different periods of time in order to become gods or goddesses. So, if I understand this correctly, the longer I stay silent, the better chance I have of becoming a goddess.

Who am I kidding? I start to make noises to remind myself I can still speak. I'm not about to become a monk anytime soon, or in this lifetime even.

There is something to this silence, though. The less I speak, the more I think. In this treehouse, no household noises pollute my thoughts. This makes me feel absent from the world, yet present in the moment. My mind begins to feel cleansed. In the treehouse, I don't have anxiety, attention-deficit/hyperactivity disorder (ADHD), or obsessive-compulsive disorder (OCD). The treehouse has grown into a safe house for my soul.

The wind is more rigorous now. We sway. I feel like I'm in a sea fort or on a boat, out in the middle of the ocean.

But like when I was taking a cold shower outside as a kid, I can be wherever I want to be. My imagination soars. It feels as though the treehouse is lifting up into the air. It might be the wind, or it might be the wine, or maybe it is both the wind and wine. Whatever this is, I'll stay and enjoy the ride for as long as it's here.

As I lay me down to sleep, I gaze at the ceiling, covered with a maroon and gray tapestry. The speakers have been strategically placed in metal paint cans, which hang below the hidden birds carved into the headboard of my twin bed. I stare into the colors on the ceiling and see twinkle lights glowing through little elephants.

The elephants have luggage on their backs. All of my problems are in the bags and bundles on the elephants' backs. I'm not hallucinating; the elephants are printed into the material. The wind, mixed with the beautiful sounds and my heightened level of creativity, can make the elephants move. They travel off the tapestry with their belongings and fly out the tear in the plastic sheeting I call the front door.

As I lie here, full of dreams and aspirations, I think of the experiences I've had, and the life yet to come. My eyes are wide with wonder. The roof blows away without a sound, and I see the stars and stare.

These are my eyes, and this is my mind. Visualization helped me survive the horrible happenings that came my way. There was always a roof, but when I looked up, I could see the sky.

The blue truck that we used to haul water

The dome in winter

Me at four years old

CHAPTER TWO

Through the Lens of a Smoke-Filled Treehouse

I was born in Indio, California, on the third of April in 1973. There were three other Jennifers born on the same day, which leads me to wonder if I might have been switched at birth. I think I had a lovely birth, but I don't remember any of it. I did, however, see a picture of myself at three weeks old, and I looked happy.

I also have a newspaper picture of when my mother had taken me to the public pool for swimming lessons. Unfortunately, the newspaper got my name wrong, but I know it's me. My mother looked thin for just having birthed me, and she seemed as happy as someone could be.

I arrived home from the hospital to an older sister named Gina. Gina was a year and a half old when I was born. We lived in a modest home in La Quinta Cove. We had a large, grassy backyard.

From what I can tell, my mom and dad were kind to my sister and me, although I don't remember any of this. Videos of my dad giving us rides on a motorcycle around the backyard tell me that what I believe is the truth. In the same footage, my sister chases a scraggly dog around the house as she laughs. We looked like we were happy children. We had a marvelous swing set and cuddly rabbits we couldn't pick up because of their razor-sharp claws. A picture also exists of me in a pretty dress with a humongous candy cane in my hand and a genuine smile on my face.

My earliest thoughts of Gina were that I was her plaything. She had short, chestnut brown hair and big brown eyes. She was huge compared to me. At the time, I didn't know what a sumo wrestler was, but if I did, that is the way I would have seen her—big, burly, and robust. I think she may have taken my food sometimes.

I was a delicate child with colorless, wispy hair and turquoise, puzzled eyes. Both my mother and father had brown hair and brown eyes. The only resemblance between Gina and me was our bowl haircut provided by our mom. Besides that, I did not look like anyone in my family, but you could tell Gina belonged to our parents.

Everywhere Gina went, I followed. She wanted to boss me around in return. Once, she had me climb into the front of a plastic toy shopping cart, and my legs became stuck. My circulation was cut off, so my dad had to cut the basket to get me out. He said it was a good thing he knew how to work with tools, or I would be stuck in that cart forever.

My parents would bowl every Friday night. They were in a league together. Their association was called The Friday Night Owls. My mom was so good she had her own shoes and ball. My dad wasn't at her skill level but always seemed to win the money shots. They were a good team and sometimes won prizes. This was their weekly night out. My sister and I frequented the bowling alley daycare. I wouldn't leave Gina's side; I felt distressed without her. As a scaredy-cat, I admired her strength.

One night, she went to the restroom, and I raced after her. When I tried to follow her in, my attempt was thwarted with force. She slammed the door shut with my hand in it. Chaos unfolded. Blood was everywhere. But the scene, which had transformed into an absolute horror show, thanks to my three-year-old eyes, was suddenly brightened by the people around me. Everyone was incredibly kind. Their concern for my welfare made me the center of attention.

The caregivers banged on the bathroom door, but my sister decided to take her time and finish her business before she opened it. She had no idea what she had done. When she finally stepped out of the restroom, she took in the grisly scene. The expression on her face, pale and scared, looked exactly how I felt. My pinky finger had nearly been chopped off. It dangled, attached only by the skin. After being rushed to the hospital, my tiniest finger was sewn back onto my hand. Today, the finger works fine.

My parents quit the league because of what happened. They took a financial blow and couldn't trust the caregivers to watch over us properly. My parents didn't sue the bowling alley, because back then, people weren't as sue-happy as they are today. They just understood and accepted that accidents happened.

WHEN I WAS ALMOST THREE years old, my baby brother was born. My dad held him often. I see now my dad probably wanted a boy so that his son could follow in his footsteps. I think the happiness my dad had about his expanding family was more significant because he now had a son.

My sister and I played with him when we could, and both our parents cared for him. He was the sweetest baby ever. We named him Jason. He had soft, curly brown hair and brown eyes. He smiled and laughed, sat upright, and held his bottle. Our family appeared perfect in the pictures we had … until the scene in front of the images transformed.

When my brother was three months old, our lives changed forever. Horror and chaos replaced all that was once predictable. My mom's screams could be heard throughout the house; her uncontrollable sobs followed. We heard my dad yell, in an ironic effort, to calm her down. Gina and I were scared and confused as we watched our brother shake. Strange noises whimpered from his mouth, and his eyes rolled back in his head.

The day before this nightmare, my brother had received his DTP shot. This vaccine was supposed to protect a baby from diphtheria, tetanus, and pertussis. These shots were vital. All babies received them.

My parents rushed us into the car; they had no insurance to afford an ambulance. We were in our pajamas. My mom held Jason in her lap as my dad drove. She thought my brother was dying. My sister and I didn't know what dying meant, but it looked terrible.

We reached the hospital, and the doctor told my parents that my brother was having grand mal seizures. My mom mentioned that Jason had just received his baby shots, but the doctor assured her the two were not related.

A team of doctors tried to count the seizures. Once they reached 150, they stopped counting. The seizures just continued. It was horrifying for everyone, especially our parents. Imagine thinking your child is about to die and no one has any idea why.

Even though we were young, my sister and I stayed out of the way and stared, with fear and confusion in our eyes, when the seizures would start. My sister and I only went to the hospital the first time this happened. After that, whenever my parents needed to take Jason to the hospital, we were not allowed to go.

The doctors told my parents that my brother would not live to see his fifth birthday. My sister and I could sense their broken hearts. The change in them was beyond words I could convey at the time, but our tiny hearts felt it firmly, and our lives changed forever.

I feel the need to stress how hard this chapter is for me. I'm in my treehouse with my left hand over my mouth, as my eyes well up with tears. None have yet trickled out because I force them back. As an adult, I see and understand all of this differently than I could as a child. To see it and write about this experience now is so necessary but utterly heartbreaking for me. I know I will revisit unresolved pain as I write this chapter, but I must face the truth about my life to understand myself and heal. And if it can help anyone, I will risk it all. I cannot hold back. I'll type through the tears.

So, the floodgates open, and my emotions soar. I smoke some pot because I don't want to go into the house for wine, where people will see my tear-streaked face. Marijuana makes me feel relaxed and creative. Wine makes me feel sophisticated. Together, they help me feel relaxed, creative, and sophisticated—an excellent combination to form a healthy foundation for storytelling.

Through my smoke-filled treehouse, a memory of my dad manifests into reality. He sits on the same recliner he has owned as long as I can remember. He holds my baby brother, who rests his right cheek on my dad's chest. That chest was strong once. Now it seems concave. My brother faces upward as he rests and looks at my dad. No, he looks past my dad, up into space. He seems to have lost his will and ability to move after a day of seizures. His face is red. The redness is blurry, so I can't tell exactly how bad the rash has become. The redness has a sheen to it as if an ointment had been applied to calm it down. His mouth is open, and drool spills over the bottom of his chapped lip. I can tell, from this profile view, that his eyes are glossy—he has been crying.

He looks like a miserable baby. His arms lie paralyzed to his sides. He doesn't move because he can't. His hair is brushed on the top of his head into a smooth wisp, like the picture of the Gerber Baby.

He is dressed in a light blue jumpsuit and white socks. He is three months old. He will never be a happy baby. He will never walk or talk. My baby brother will die before he is five years old.

My dad is shaggy. If I were a cartoonist, that is the thing I would make stand out the most. He never used to be this hairy. He has dark brown hair above his lip, on the sides of his face, and on his cheeks and chin. His beard is not mountain-man length, but it is a sure sign of shaving neglect, as if he just stopped grooming altogether. A strong aura lingers around his chair and suggests this too. Or perhaps the Mary Jane cloud in the treehouse has misled my vision.

My eyes begin to bemuse me. Whatever the nimbus is, it signifies the passing of a distressed ego. A man's identity unrestrictedly being let go, because it has no place here anymore. One energy must be replaced by another, though. He is now the epitome of altruism. A machine, once a man with dreams, aspirations, and explanations, now irrecoverable.

The hair on his head matches the hair on his face, of course. It is a mess and hasn't been brushed for days. Imagine Einstein on a bad hair day, but worse. His back is one with the recliner. His gray T-shirt is wrinkled. His right arm mimics my brother's—straight down and paralyzed. His legs are in worn jeans and they, too, are paralyzed.

It is strange how sometimes the look on a face can be harder to describe than the meaning in someone's eyes. I could interpret my dad's expression, convert it into emotions, but I don't want to. Better to observe with an emotionless, clinical eye. He's dehydrated. Too much beer is the likely culprit.

His eyes, though, stare past the camera. A candid picture tells so much more than one that is posed. All illusions fade away. My father, without a façade, is difficult to look at. His eyes aren't completely vacant, but something is not right. Did he not know he was supposed to smile for the camera? Did he not know his photo was being taken? Or did he simply not care? In his averted gaze, I see the fall of a man— an exhausted, confused, and defeated man—financially drained with hundreds of thousands of dollars in debt, two small daughters, and now a severely disabled baby boy under his care. The exhibition was undeniably the gaze of a man with newfound alcohol addiction, and a wife who was about to lose her mind.

CHAPTER THREE

Boots, Beer, and A.1. Sauce

We are now abandoned by our own blood. Eating condiments to survive. Pushed out of the circle we once completed. Day after day, the madness repeated.

Rain falls gently as I walk toward the treehouse, now enveloped in a dense fog. I can see where I step, but I have no idea where I will take you tonight. I am a fly-by-the-seat-of-my-pants type of girl at times.

The first thing I do when I enter the treehouse is greet the surge protector, and hope he doesn't quit on me during my stay. The surge protector is connected to a long, yellow extension cord. The yellow cord is attached to a long, once-bright-orange, now rustic-looking extension cord. The rustic cord is plugged into a grimy outlet on the outside of the house. The connections have met. I climb the ladder and flip the switch on the surge protector, and the treehouse comes alive as if to say "Welcome, Jennifer."

The rain taps the sheet-metal roof. The Christmas lights glow, the heater coils ignite, the wine is poured, the lights are low, the music is just right. I am physically alone as I prepare to enter the depths of my mind. Somehow, I feel safe with you here.

Are you ready? Hold my hand. Let's fly into the mist and over the light. The rain is warm, the moon is bright. Spread your arms and fly with me. You will not know what you never see.

My world changed overnight; all attention was on my brother now. A new family developed before my eyes, consisting of my mom, my dad, and my brother. My sister and I were no longer involved; we had no place. We were not a priority because we were healthy. In our home, *normal children* were a nuisance.

The next few years would play out like a heartbreaking *Groundhog Day* scene. The impact this new drama had on my parents was tremendous. My dad no longer smiled or laughed. My mom cried all day long and played records, and if she saw us come out of our room while my dad was home after work, she would whisper loudly, "Get back in the room!" We listened and did what we were told because we wanted her to be happy. For whatever reason, she didn't want us around our dad.

I took the whole situation worse than my sister, which would be apparent to you if you knew her. My sister took care of herself, whereas I felt like the needy one. I was only three; my sister was four, going on five.

Gina was busy at play as if life was wonderful. I was very curious as to what was happening. If I asked her too many questions, she would eventually get upset with me. I became the whiny, needy little sister she was too young to comfort. She just wanted to be left alone. She didn't even want to play with me anymore.

My dad was an auto-body man, and my mom took care of my brother all day. If my brother had a seizure while my dad was at work, my mom would drop us off at a babysitter's house. After work, my dad would meet my mom at the hospital. The hospital was called Loma Linda. My dad said the drive was long, but it was the best hospital around.

Sometimes we were with the babysitter for days. I often wished we could stay there forever because there were new toys and other children to play with. What I liked most was that somebody came to check on me if I cried, and if we were hungry, we were given food.

We were allowed to roam freely, but I never felt like the other kids. I would usually just sit and stare at them. I liked to watch how they played, and I sometimes wished I was them, or that this was my house and my family. Eventually, my parents would come for us, we would go home, and the fantasy would end.

As for Gina and me, we dressed ourselves and were helped by no one. My mom told us children were meant to be seen and not heard. I didn't have any idea what she was talking about. If I asked a question, she wouldn't answer, so I usually just went away. I felt so sad and alone. I felt like she didn't like me. I felt abandoned and confused. I knew I was a burden and an inconvenience.

When I say abandoned, I *do not* mean in the harshest form of the word. My mom made some efforts to communicate with my sister and me. But she neglected to provide care, support, and supervision for us. This was unintentional. Unfortunately, I cannot come up with a diagnosis for this; I'm not a clinical psychologist. I will call it "accidental abandonment." She forgot about us the way some people forget they left their children in a hot car because their minds were elsewhere. What she did was similar to this.

My mom became instantly insane the night my brother had the first seizure; I am sure of this. She became a different person overnight. She exhibited what I now know to be extreme depression, anxiety, mood swings, insomnia, and detachment. She once cared about her looks, but after Jay Jay's seizures, she wouldn't even brush her hair or shower and would wear the same clothes again and again. She also became codependent. She began to sacrifice her own needs to take care of my brother.

She also developed a martyr complex. My mom always blamed God for my brother's disabilities. She told us that God cursed her and wanted her to suffer. She often complained about how her life was over because of my brother. Most days, she moped around the house and blamed others for everything that went wrong. Yet she was always there for Jay Jay.

So far, I have diagnosed my mom with a few mental illnesses. Perhaps, in a way, I have done this to protect myself from thinking a perfectly sane person would ever treat her own children like this. The mental illnesses were real. If they weren't, I would not have been able to understand any of this, and it would be a challenge to write this book.

The impact of my thoughts hits me as I write; I now begin to wonder if this is a book or a public journal. Right now, I know a three-year-old girl, and I love her and cannot imagine her on her own asking unanswered questions with no adults to help her. No matter what the circumstances were, I would never be able to tell her to go away. I would have to be mental. I imagine her helpless face, and it breaks my heart.

Did my mom suddenly snap or was she always like this? Unfortunately, I can't remember anything before the age of three; I just see pictures. In the photographs, everything seemed impressive, but was it?

Answers were needed. A couple of days ago, I spoke to my dad on the phone to make sure some facts were straight for my book. I felt nervous calling him. I usually only call him to wish him a happy birthday or to borrow money.

It shattered my heart to hear that before the night of my brother's seizures, my mom really was a different person. My dad told me she was happy and funny. She had dreams; she wanted to be a flight attendant. She was thin and took care of herself. She was nice.

"Was Mom proud of us?" I asked. "Did she dress us in pretty clothes?"

"She did," he said.

"Did she love us?"

"Yes!"

He is a man of few words, who rarely elaborates. I started to cry when I imagined this once-perfect family.

"Do you think Mom lost her mind after the night of Jason's first seizures? Did she become a different person?"

18

There was a pause before he answered. "Yes."

It was the most awkward conversation I have ever had in my life with anyone. There were a lot of quiet moments. I was quiet; he was quiet.

Then I blurted out the question I was dying to ask. "Did you become an alcoholic because of what happened or did you already drink that much?"

Silence.

"Hello? Hello?"

He eventually replied, his voice barely audible, "Yes, I drank a lot more to relax."

After an awkward silence, I asked, "To relax or to escape the situation? I mean, you now had a mentally disabled son who might die at any moment, a crazy wife, and two young daughters to care for, and bills and debt and …"

He was silent for a long time as we both thought about everything else I didn't mention. He probably contemplated hanging up on me, but before he could, I said, "I believe you were an alcoholic because you would give me a penny for every beer I brought you at night, and sometimes I would have a handful of pennies at the end of the night."

He said nothing, but I heard his breath, so I continued, "I don't judge you at all. I understand. I never saw you as an alcoholic because you were never mean. At the time, I thought alcoholics were mean."

I continued, "Did you ever know what went on when you were at work?"

Silence.

"Mom cried all day and listened to Kenny Rogers. When you came home, she would shut off the records, wipe her eyes, and tell us to get in the back room."

Still silence.

"You would come in, and she would only focus on you and Jay Jay, and she never fed us dinner. Gina would sneak into the kitchen at night and get the A.1. Sauce, and we would share it. We tried the other condiments too, but they were nasty. A.1. Sauce was like a meal.

Mom yelled at us once because it was all gone when she was giving you steak. So, from then on, Gina would fill the bottle back up with water, and you would tell Mom the sauce was watery. She would have no idea why, but that's why."

There was silence for a long time, but I knew he was there. I didn't want him to feel guilty for something he didn't do, so I continued.

"Now I'm addicted to A.1. Sauce. At fancy restaurants, I ask for it and they look at me like I'm crazy to ruin a perfect steak."

He laughed, and so did I.

I DON'T BLAME MY DAD. I don't think he ever even knew we were home, even though I was always sitting about twelve feet away, staying out of sight so my mom wouldn't see me. We were not allowed to be seen when he came home, so I hid between the fireplace and the hall, with my back straight against the wall. If anyone had to go to the bathroom, I would close my eyes and become one with the wall, and no one would see me. I sat there all night, watching and wishing I could be a part of what was now one fucked-up little family. I didn't know the f-word then, but it fits appropriately now. I didn't care how messed up it was, I just wanted to be included. I was lonely. My mom made it clear that we were no longer a priority.

They say it takes eight days to get used to change. My sister and I got used to this way of life fast. Interaction between anyone in our house was sparse. Gina was ever-elusive. She could have been living with another family down the road and no one would have noticed. Perhaps she was playing house in the back room or digging underground tunnels. As for me, I watched my mom and dad with Jay Jay, like I was watching a strange play I'd seen a thousand times. If my brother didn't spend the night at Loma Linda, my dad came home. When we saw him pull up to the house, we would holler, "He's here! He's here!"

My mom would scurry toward us as fast as she could and tell us to stay in the back and not come into the living room. So, we ran. We couldn't even say hello to him anymore. He couldn't hear us if we did anyway. He had selective hearing, and us girls were not selected to be heard.

We used to greet him all the time. Gina and I would run and sit on his feet. He had big, brown work boots. He would give us a ride on his feet as he walked. We would laugh; it was so much fun. I was sad we couldn't do that anymore, and I wondered when we could do it again.

Maybe this is why I occasionally run to the door yelling, "Daddy!" when some of the men I've dated come home. I jump on them and tell them how much I've missed them. I kiss them and make them feel as special as I can. Then I run and disappear because that is a bit strange for a grown woman to be doing, and I don't want them to think I'm crazy. Yet they always seem to like it.

My dad came home each night after a long day at work worn out and quiet. I would stare at him to see if he did something different, but his routine was always the same. He walked in with his head down, and if he didn't go to the bathroom first, he would fall into his recliner and let out a sigh.

Whenever my dad came home, my mom transformed. She stopped crying, shuddered away her tears, and turned off her melancholy Kenny Rogers record, which had been wearing the needle down from repeated plays. She moved faster. She would tap her fingers, looking like she wanted to speak while remaining silent. Dutifully, my mother would turn the television to the news, bring my father dinner on a tray, and stand there, waiting like a servant. If my father ever rose from his upholstered throne, my mother would observe him carefully, terrified that she had done something wrong.

She would panic and ask what was wrong. She would follow him, trying not to trip over her own feet. He wouldn't answer; he just walked to the kitchen, with her chasing behind him, and opened the fridge.

He would return to his chair, crack his beer, take a drink, and take off his boots. She would stand there, staring at him like she was an assistant and he was a tyrant. I don't know why she did this; he wasn't mean. She was nervous; she was always shaky and didn't finish sentences.

When he took the first bite of his meal, she would ask, "Is it okay? Is it okay? Huh, Wes, huh? Is it okay?" He wouldn't answer but instead would stare at the TV. My mom would repeat, "Is it okay? Wes? Wes?"

When she spoke, I mouthed her words. It was the same every time. It was like watching a movie a million times; it became entertaining. My favorite part to mouth was when he finally had enough and yelled, "Goddammit, woman!"

She would scurry off into the kitchen to feed my brother, and that scene would end. I would cover my mouth and try not to laugh. I would stare at my dad as he sat in his chair. He looked different. He didn't talk a lot. He only yelled when my mom started panicking over my brother.

One night, he saw that I was there, watching. After a few minutes, he said, "Jenny. Beer." He began to do this every night. I would run and get a beer, so excited to be involved again. When I brought it to him, he would give me a penny. I became so excited that I would run to our room and hide the coin, and run right back to my post, hoping I'd get another opportunity to be involved.

My mood became entirely dependent on my parents, even though I wasn't allowed to be a part of their lives. I wanted to be involved so badly that I would watch my dad drink his current beer, and when he neared the end with his head tilted back, I would become like a runner, waiting to hear the starter pistol. After he said, "Jenny," but before he said, "beer," I was halfway to the refrigerator.

Finally, I was needed—needed in a way that I felt like I was a part of the family. It gave me a pattern to follow. There was a sense of pride that came with the job, too, even though I was essentially a four-year-old cocktail waitress. Soon after, more jobs came. I would be responsible for unlacing my dad's boots when he got home. Once the laces were undone, I had to pull back with all my strength to get the boots off, an effort that always resulted in me falling back, onto my butt. The socks were a less enjoyable task. They were usually wet and smelled rotten. I would pull them off as quickly as possible, throw them, and run away screaming. This nightly ritual formed a tiny world I loved, the world of "boots, beer, and A.1. Sauce."

Things were beginning to look up. My brother started a medication that helped control his seizures, and he began intense physical therapy to gain muscle strength. My mom made friends with a Jehovah's Witness black lady from down the road who had a couple of kids. My dad didn't lose his mind, and he came home every night, like clockwork. I became his official boot taker-offer. The extended family started visiting and would sometimes take us on outings. And my sister and I were thrilled to find out we were now of age to leave the house and roam the streets alone. Yeah, life was good. But I would soon discover I was not prepared for what the outside world had in store for me.

Gina and me on Halloween

CHAPTER FOUR

Munchausen, Miracles, and Me

The role of patient was an intimate and soothing one, for I did not care to know what the role of child was any longer.

"The Butterfly Sky Escape"
Warm flowing air and a butterfly breeze,
We spin as we point toward the hills in the mist.
Sparks start to shoot from our pink fingertips.
Butterflies fall into waves that freeze.
Ice is now art, at the edge of our feet;
We ice skate upon the breathtaking sight.
The ice starts to crackle, but we feel no fright.
The wings set upon our small backs as we rise,
Ice skating butterflies now fill the skies.
–Jennifer Asbenson

I'm upside down. We are spinning in circles; my arms are out. My face beams with euphoria. I'm like a bird, no worries on my mind. My feet are tightly held in hands a few years older than mine. I scream with joy, but I feel the hands slip, and I fly head-first into the cement. I'm dead in their eyes; then I come to. I am loved. Little bluebirds fly around my head in circles, chirping. I'm dazed and confused. They rush me home, and my mom calls the doctor. The doctor says I should be fine as long as I do not throw up. As she starts to speak, I begin to vomit. "Take her to the hospital immediately." So, she does.

As I sit here in my treehouse, I feel warm and cozy. Hot cocoa swirls in my cup while little marshmallows dance around on top. *Why does telling the next part of the story make me feel so comfortable?* Perhaps it is because this was the first time I felt love. In reality, what I felt was not love. My brain was deceived to believe it was, so I would feel like a worthy human being. I needed to feel cared for and nurtured.

This may sound twisted, but I liked the attention. Even though those concerned eyes and caring hands were a result of my being physically hurt, I wanted more. People would actually look at me. They would hold me, talk to me. In those moments, I would pretend the doctors and nurses were my parents. They were kind to me. A definition for "hurt" formed in my mind. It made me feel special, happy, and warm. My ideas of love and pain had been swapped, blended. I enjoyed getting hurt; I wanted to get hurt all the time, even if I had to help the process along.

AFTER I WAS RUSHED TO the hospital, tests were performed. The doctor decided to operate because I had a bad brain bleed. All eyes were on me. There were many mothers and fathers (a.k.a. nurses and doctors), all helpful and caring. It would break their hearts if I were to die. They didn't want me to die, just like my mom didn't want my brother to die. I wondered why there was no crying and screaming. They were all calm.

And they all loved me: the doctors, the nurses, everyone. Warm blankets were draped over me, and I was showered in love. They brought me food. They talked to me and asked me questions; my answers were important to them.

Before surgery, a technician did one more scan to see if the crack in my brain had changed. It had. My brain stopped bleeding, just like that. I was discharged the next morning, and my *lovefest* ended. That was when I decided to try and get hurt or play sick as often as I could, so I could feel love.

By age four, I had Munchausen syndrome. Thirty-nine years later, I would diagnose myself in my treehouse. Munchausen syndrome is associated with severe neglect and abuse. A person pretends to be sick or will hurt her body in order to visit the hospital to feel cared for and loved.

I had a lighter form of Munchausen because I was not severely neglected. I was only pushed aside and left out. For me, this was enough to leave an impact at such a young age. Most children are afraid to get hurt. I began to hope I would become injured so that I could experience what I believed was love.

Any chance I could, I wanted to get hurt. The hospital meant love. It made me feel special to go there. I adored the cleanliness, the smell, the food, and the affection. If any little thing happened to me, I would cry, overreact, and say I needed to go to the hospital, even if I didn't feel pain. I would also become a daredevil in an attempt to get hurt. With my luck, I'd usually perfect the stunt before I'd get hurt.

I was now four, and my sister was five. We were allowed to go outside and play on our own. My mom always told us to watch out for cars; we had no other rules. We would roam the neighborhood. We met some kids down the road who had a secret freezer in their garage full of the most delicious snacks: donuts, pink Sno Balls, ice cream, all the fantastic junk food imaginable. Sometimes they would let us have one. I would climb on a chair and lean into the gigantic, frosty deep freezer and feel the ice-cold air hit my skin. I would blow into the freezer and say "ahhhh" as the fog swept away to expose the surprises beneath. I'd suddenly feel awake and excited. The neighbor boy would tell me to hurry before everything melted. I would get anxious, bite my bottom lip, and wiggle my fingers in hopes they would grab a treat on their own so I wouldn't have to choose. Still, I would always change my mind once the boy began to shut the lid.

We also met older kids who lived down the block. That is where I flew like a bird and felt euphoric … before my face kissed the pavement. My mom said only a stupid kid with no brains would swing a toddler upside down by their feet for fun. We never saw those kids again after my trip to the hospital.

One day, my mom came home and told us she met a friend. We took a walk to her house. My brother was in a stroller. He was now one year old. For some reason, he never wore pants, only a large saggy diaper with a shirt full of drool. He still could not crawl, walk, or talk. He could kick and throw, though, but only while he was sitting or lying down.

Gina and I were excited to go to someone's house. We never walked with my mom to anyone's house, so this was special. We were greeted at the door by a loud lady named Mary. She was lovely and said hello to us; her three children bounced with anticipation in the background. Her house had a musty, familiar smell—the type of smell you would unwillingly inhale while opening a hefty bag of used clothes from a stranger. A smell you don't like, but you gladly accept because of its benefits.

As my sister gleefully went off to play with the older girl, I was attacked. By that I mean Tiffany was so excited by my white skin and blond hair that her behavior resembled an assault. She grabbed my arms so that she could touch my skin. Instead of treating me like a playmate, she looked at me as if I were a doll, *her* doll. She combed her long piano fingers through my hair. Much like the toy she thought I was, I remained motionless. It was clear Tiffany was unable to control herself.

Excitement began to brew in her wide-set eyes. She repeated, "Oh, my lawd" in an awkward, high-pitched voice. At this point, I didn't know if I was going to be her new friend or her last supper. Attention was always welcomed, but this was weird. This form of love was a kind I was not accustomed to.

"Jenny, let me look at that hair. Oh, my lawd." Tiffany started to sweep my hair to one side in a calm, compassionate manner. She leaned in, as if she desired to kiss me, but instead, she took a big whiff of my hair. I was bewildered and terrified, and I wanted to leave. To cause a distraction, I dramatically pulled away and grabbed onto my brother's stroller.

My mom took notice and told us to go play in the back room. This excited Tiffany, and she grabbed me and pulled me back to see her room. My reaction was as if I were being dragged into a haunted house. I was skeptical. But at the end of the hall, I was delighted to see bunk beds and posters of a black man she called "Michael Jackson." Before I could get a closer look at the man with one white glove, my mom yelled to us that it was time to go.

As we walked out the door, Mary said, "I'm serious, Alice. The girls can spend the night here anytime."

I think that was the first time I experienced extreme anxiety. I did not want to be left alone with Tiffany. Ever!

MY BROTHER HAD BEEN PRESCRIBED medication to relax his muscles so the seizures would stop. Ironically, the doctors would do biopsies on his muscles and say, "Unfortunately, there seems to be no muscle growth."

My dad told us a lot of doctors had zero common sense, and he didn't know how they survived on a day-to-day basis. He told them to stop prescribing Jay Jay the "damn muscle relaxers" and choose something else. Once his medication was changed, Jay Jay began to acquire a significant amount of muscle growth.

By the time Jay Jay was two, he was in aggressive physical therapy. He had a beautiful angel named Esther. I have no idea where she came from; she just knocked one day. We opened the door, and my mom pushed us out of the way and told us to go to the back room. Instead, Gina and I stood near the hall because we had overheard Mom telling Dad the day before about this lady who had a crazy bag of tricks. We were excited to sneak a peek. Esther set her bag on the floor.

"I'll be right back," she said.

"You two had better stay out of the way or you'll get it later," my mom said. We stepped back in obedience.

Esther came back with a huge blue ball. She set the ball down and spoke to my mom and introduced herself to Jay Jay, which I thought was strange because he couldn't even talk. Then she turned around and looked at us.

"I'm Esther."

If she was going to say more, it would not have mattered; my mom interrupted Esther and said, "They won't be in your way."

Esther smiled. "No, I don't mind if they watch."

"You better stay out of the way," my mom warned us.

Esther was kind and gentle. I watched, day after day, as she laid Jay Jay on his belly on the massive ball while holding his arms. She pushed the ball back to let his feet touch the ground. I thought her attempts were a waste of time, but it was fun to watch. One day, she turned to me and said, "Eventually he will crawl, stand up, walk, and run." I laughed but kept my thoughts to myself. *No, he will never do that.*

On weekdays, Esther took Jay Jay swimming. She was always around. I thought she was amazing, and I loved to watch her. She was calm and optimistic. She even talked about my brother participating in the Special Olympics. When she explained the organization to me, I thought she was nuts.

One day, my brother cried and threw a fit and didn't want anything to do with Esther. He was three now. I sat behind her and watched. After a moment, I whispered, "He likes Kenny Rogers."

"Kenny Rogers? Do you like Kenny Rogers?" she asked Jay Jay in a baby voice. "Where is Kenny Rogers, Jenny?"

I pointed at the record player. Her excitement made me feel special, but I was also nervous because we were not allowed to touch my mom's records.

"Well, let's give Jay Jay some Kenny Rogers then."

I just looked at her.

"Jenny, do you know how to put the record on?"

"I can't."

"Would you like to be my helper? Would you put Kenny Rogers on every day for your brother?"

I was so excited to be needed. "You have to ask my mom. She doesn't let us touch them."

My mom overheard and walked into the room. "I don't want the kids touching my records."

"Can I help her put Kenny Rogers on?" Esther asked. "I will take full responsibility."

My mom reluctantly agreed. By six years old, I was a cocktail waitress and a DJ.

Esther showed up, day after day. We would play the Kenny Rogers record, and my brother would laugh and want to dance. Eventually, he pushed with his legs. Jay Jay improved with each passing day. Esther would move the ball as if he were going to fall off, and he would catch himself with his hands. We watched Jay Jay gain strength, and I felt proud to be a part of this work.

As I entered kindergarten, Esther continued to grace us with her kindness and persistence. Her efforts paid off. One day, out of the blue, Jay Jay scooted on his belly to the TV and pulled himself up. He stood on his own! My sister grabbed his legs, and Jay Jay put his hands on the floor. We could walk him like a wheelbarrow. This was hilarious to us! We could hold his legs and go fast, and he would never fall. Those little arms were crazy quick. When we weren't holding his legs, he would crawl everywhere. It was somewhat scary, though, because he never crawled on his knees. He squirmed around with his legs straight, butt in the air, and arms straight. We called him "Stink Bug." He moved with impressive speed.

Life improved as my brother gained strength and ability. On the weekends, we would go to the car races. I loved the sights and the sounds. We strapped Jay Jay down with strong Velcro my dad brought home from work so my brother wouldn't buck himself out of his stroller. My dad said there was no way he could break out of that. Gina and I fed him junk food and entertained him with funny faces so he wouldn't make noises and disturb others. The car races provided enjoyment, a rarity in our lives.

ONCE, MY GRANDMA AND AUNT on my mom's side came for a visit. This was the first time I felt admiration. My grandmother never yelled like my mom; she spoke softly. She stood tall and moved with grace. She had manners, and she seemed interested in us. My Aunt Janine captivated me. She was a couple years younger than my mom but looked the complete opposite. She had blond hair, recently brushed, and light-colored eyes like mine. I thought she resembled me. She wore a bit of makeup and clean, wrinkle-free clothes that made her even prettier. She had a beautiful New York accent that sounded fancy. I'd glance at my slouched-over, grumpy-faced mom and then look at Aunt Janine and wonder how they could be related and yet so different. My mom exuded negativity, but Janine was positive. It was like comparing the darkness to the sun. Sometimes I wished Janine was my mom.

Before they came over for their visit, my mom told us not to ask my aunt or grandma for anything. We had all we needed, she told us, and we didn't need handouts from people who thought they were better than us. Besides, Janine stole my mom's baseball cards when they were kids, and she was still upset about that. It confused me to imagine Janine could be capable of doing such a thing, considering how much my mom loved those damn Mets.

My mom seemed angry when she talked about Janine. It didn't make me like her any less, though. Janine and my grandma treated us well. They even took us to a store. I usually wasn't allowed to go because if I saw parents being nice to their children, I would beg them to take me home with them. Sometimes I would have to be pried off their baskets and pulled to our car, crying the whole way. Since I wasn't allowed to ask Janine and my grandma if I could go home with them or have any of their money, I continued to ask strangers when they took us out.

When Janine and my grandma left, my mom gave us an earful.

"You girls know that Janine only has money because she doesn't have kids to take care of, right?" Gina and I could only stare at our mom. We didn't dare respond.

"And if she did have kids, she would never be able to handle a disabled child," my mom said. "Cursed people don't get to pick and choose their paths like Janine can."

My sister and I sat in silence.

"Janine has a good job working for the government, and she doesn't have any brats to tie her down." My mom's voice grew louder. "Her life is perfect! She has no idea what the real world is like!"

After a few moments, my mom calmed down. When she spoke next, there was a hint of sadness in her voice. "Janine was coddled. She was treated so well by your grandma. But not me. My mom even hit me with her high-heel shoe once, hard enough that the heel broke right off!"

I didn't care about anything my mom said. I still would have left with my grandma and my aunt if they had invited me.

ONE TIME, I ASKED A pretty girl in kindergarten if I could live with her. She said yes, so we got on the bus together, and I was dropped off with her at her house. Her mother had no idea who I was. I asked if I could live there. I didn't even know my last name. No one knew where I was or what to do. I didn't care; the girl and I dressed up in all of her pretty clothes for hours. Her room was like a princess castle. Her mom fed us lovely food on a flowery dinner plate. The pretty girl just ate it. I took a picture of it with my eyes first. The food was art, not dinner. I sat and ate and hoped I'd never be found. Unfortunately, after many phone calls, everything was figured out. But it was late, so I got to spend the night and wear her amazing, beautiful, clean clothes to school in the morning.

Now, let me tell you a scary story. You know by now that I derail, then always get back on track. No way you were going to slip by without reading this part.

One day, my mom made an announcement. "Jay Jay is with Grandma, and Dad and I are going on a date. You two girls get to spend the night at Mary's house."

My heart dropped, and a feeling of doom hit me. The thought of Tiffany sniffing my hair again terrified me. I imagined her setting up a torture chamber just for me.

When we arrived, Mary said, "We are going to eat dinner now. Then we are going to get ready to go to the Jehovah's Witnesses meeting."

Mary was tough, so everybody ran to the table, and I followed. I had no clue what was on the plate.

Her son asked, "What's this, Ma?" Mary slapped his mouth.

I tried not to cry because I thought the food on my plate was fish, and I hated fish.

"Come on, Jenny, eat your fish," Mary said.

I was afraid. "I need a drink."

"Oh, no. No one gets a drink until after they eat all their dinner. That's the rule here."

The other children began to eat against their will. They looked motivated by fear, so I ate. Then Mary gave us milk. I drank mine so fast, the milk came out of my nose. My nerves crippled me, and I dropped my cup on the table, knocking over someone else's milk.

"Slow down, Jenny," Mary said. "Haven't you ever eaten at a dinner table before?"

I actually hadn't, but I had no time to answer. Tiffany grabbed me before I could wipe my milk mustache.

"It's hair time, Jenny!" She whisked me to the bathroom and pulled out her hair kit of horrors. "Where's the hot iron?"

She made me sit on the floor, and I felt like she was trying to pull my head off by my hair. She started digging aimlessly in the cabinet with one hand, while holding my hair in the other. The words *hot iron* played over and over in my head. Was she going to burn my hair off with this hot iron? How hot was it? I felt terrified, and no one was around to help me. I sat there, held my ears, and tried not to cry.

She dipped her hand in Vaseline and started to part my hair and twist and pull. The rubber bands snapped here and there. I smelled heat from the apparatus in her hand, but I never looked at it. I didn't want to get burned.

"Oh, you're going to look so beautiful, Jenny." Tiffany spoke in a strange voice, as if she had waited her whole life to do this. Ten minutes later, we were all done.

My entire head felt numb. She helped me stand and said, "Now, look how beautiful you are." I looked in the mirror. My eyes were slits that almost touched my ears. I had a headache. A gazillion tiny lines zigzagged all over my head. When I tried to touch my head, Tiffany slapped my hand away.

"Uh-uh!" she said. She put more Vaseline on my hair and sprayed my head with hair spray.

Mary yelled down the hallway, "Time to go!"

We all walked down the road to the Jehovah's Witnesses meeting. I could hardly see through my venetian blinds for eyes. I started to think about an escape plan. When the meeting ended, we walked home. Afterward, Tiffany danced to Michael Jackson. I eventually fell asleep while sitting upright on the floor.

Suddenly, all was silent and I was in a warm bath. I opened my eyes and wondered what had happened. The room was dark. I saw Tiffany asleep on the top bunk. I looked down to see that I had peed on the floor. In a panic, I gathered my things, snuck out the back door, walked all the way home, and slept on the back porch. I was found alive the next day around noon, huddled in a ball, with a dirty doormat for a blanket. That was the last time I ever spent the night at Tiffany's.

A few weeks later, I rode on the handlebars of a neighbor boy's bike and got my foot caught in the spokes. He was the boy with the freezer full of ice cream. The experience was pleasant, in a way, because his parents gave me free ice cream, and I took a trip to the hospital again. The doctor said that my ankle was sprained, and I'd have to stay off of it for several days. While they wrapped my foot, I cried so that I would receive more love and affection. I thought if I cried with all my might, they would let me stay, but they didn't. My mom took me home and lectured me about my clumsiness and carelessness. I was selfish, she said, because I forced her and my dad to pay extra hospital bills they could not afford.

"Miraculous Misery"
Not one experience has ever lasted forever, like rain.
Sometimes rain comes when we are drowning
And sometimes it comes when we have a drought.
Either way, it never stays, yet a rainbow finds its route.
A lizard, in need of a drink,
feels blessed when God sends rain.
While a rat stuck in a ditch would never see the gain.
Good for some, yet bad for others.
Misery mine,
Miracle, my brother's.

Me at four years old, pretending to bake

Me at six years old, sporting a backpack that my aunt made me

Grandma and Grandpa Asbenson

Me in kindergarten

Me in first grade

CHAPTER FIVE

Church, Buttermilk, and Responsibility

Teensy-weensy clothespins hang across the string of Christmas lights. The clothespins are placed strategically so the colorful lights will shine on the sticky notes that dangle below them. So far, there are four, soon to be five. My heart is drenched in wine as I listen to the sweet rhymes of Norah Jones. I've had a headache for ten days now. Sometimes I wonder if I have brain damage. Despite, I must write, and I will manage.

The four notes hang with their names written out. Their names
are the chapters this tree brought about. Now is your time,
number five, to arrive. Be brave, forget shame, be strong, move
along, and bleed deep.

The screams came again in the middle of the night. My mom was frantic. My dad yelled. There was a short silence after the screams, followed by cries of disbelief. When my sister and I walked into my parents' room, they passed us as they ran out. They didn't have Jay Jay. Fear gripped me as I looked into his crib. I was horrified to see that he was gone.

My sister and I began to panic, and we ran after my parents. We saw them running down the road and my brother running in front of them. Shock hit me. My brother had never walked! He could crawl and climb and get into things, but he never walked. Yet, on this night, he had decided to run. He had climbed out of his crib, opened the front door, and took off, with no destination, into the dark.

It seemed like Jay Jay wouldn't stop until caught. He was like one of those small dogs you can't let out of the house because they will run and run. When you call for them, they act like they are deaf and keep going. We once had a dog named Fritz, and he did the same thing. My brother was just like Fritz, but less hairy. He ran like a deaf dog, occasionally looking back, but never stopping.

I tried to research why disabled people run but got nowhere. So, I will admit, I looked up why small dogs run. Trust me, they do not run for the same reasons. My brother was not "in heat." So, we will leave that one alone.

My parents finally caught my brother, and as they carried him back, he acted like a fish out of water. He flailed his arms and legs in an attempt to break out of my dad's clutches. As they neared the house, I remembered that Esther said Jay Jay would run one day. I did not know it would be this soon. I stood and waited to see how my mom and dad would respond because I couldn't respond differently than they did—that wouldn't be right. I felt happy to know Jay Jay could run, but it was also scary that he ran out of the house at night!

They walked into the house and put him down, but he stiffened his legs, ran into the wall, and fell down. He picked himself up and ran into the wall again. We had to stand where we didn't want him to go. I laughed because it seemed funny. My mom and dad looked at each other with bewilderment on their faces. This continued for a few more hours. My mom turned on the TV. They sat on the couch, and my dad tried to fall asleep. I ran all over, thrilled to show off my defensive blocking skills.

"What do we do?" my mom asked my dad.

"We move."

"Where will we move to?"

"Well, we will have to move near my mom and dad into that extra trailer. They are out about two miles from paved roads. So when Jay Jay runs, we can catch him."

I knew where my grandma and grandpa lived. Their home was in a little town called Sky Valley. The town probably earned this name because the best thing to look at was the sky. All that seemed to exist in this place was dirt. They lived in the middle of nowhere. There were four trailers in the compound where they lived. Two were close to each other, so from an aerial view, they looked like a triangle. The area was surrounded by dirt, rocks, and large hills. And there were a few trees—the ugly kind of trees often found on the sides of railroad tracks to block the wind.

I thought about how I would have to go to a new school. I was seven years old and almost finished with first grade. My cousins lived on the compound somewhere, so I felt better. Also, Grandma and Grandpa were sweet. I wondered if I would ever see my friends again. What about Tiffany? What about the neighbor who liked to swing me upside down by my feet and drop me on my head? Or the kids up the road with the freezer full of ice cream in their garage—the ones who rode me on the bike handlebars and got my foot trapped in the spokes?

I had beautiful memories, and I was going to miss them all. But most of all, what about Esther? I loved her. I knew I wouldn't see her again; I felt so sad. My mom said Esther's job was done because she taught Jay Jay everything she had to offer. Her job had been to teach my brother to walk, but instead, she taught him to fly.

I know why my brother ran. Freedom, I believe—freedom from his imprisonment. Inside his brain, he secretly knew he had once been healthy. He turned everything he couldn't accomplish into one thing he could: He hit the ground running.

We packed in a hurry to move to the Sky Valley compound. In the meantime, we had to barricade all doors and windows. Jay Jay was like a fierce monkey; he spent all of his confined hours trying to get out. We did everything in our power to exhaust his energy. None of our strategies worked. My mom couldn't put him in the crib anymore. He would climb right out and run. Only a cage would keep him safe, she said, but that would be considered child abuse.

The only way for him to fall asleep was to take a ride in the car. My mom, my brother, and I drove around town all night in the brown Mazda station wagon, trying to get him to fall asleep. My mom would stare straight while in a daze. I never knew what she was thinking. I always focused on the beautiful streetlights and houses and imagined amazing things until I fell asleep.

One night, as we drove up and down the streets, I saw a beautiful house I had never noticed before. My mom slowed down in front of the gray and white home. While I peered out the window at the house, and before I had time to let my mind run free, I was startled to see a mom, dad, and a small child rush to our car. My mom rolled down the passenger window.

The man put his head inside the car. "Is that Jenny? Jenny, is that you?"

"Yes," I whispered, careful not to wake my brother beside me in the backseat.

"Come inside. Live with us. It's okay with your mom. She's got a lot on her hands."

I looked at my mom. She smiled and nodded her head, but I did not move. I just sat there.

"Jenny, Jenny. Come on," the man said.

Then his voice started to change. "Jenny, come on!"

He grabbed me and started shaking me. "Jenny, come on. I put your brother in the house already. He fell asleep."

My eyes opened quickly. I should have known it was only a dream. I snuck into the house and went to sleep, hoping the dream would continue.

WE SAID OUR GOOD-BYES TO everyone and moved into a white double-wide trailer at the top of the compound's triangle. It was the farthest from civilization and sat higher than the others, so we could see the dirt roads if my brother took off. The nearest public place was a church. There were a couple of houses scattered between the compound and the church.

My grandparents lived in a tiny travel trailer. Their trailer was closest to ours and always smelled like vinegar. My grandma boiled it all the time for some reason. I thought she was trying to get rid of evil spirits or something. Apparently, it helped my grandpa's breathing.

Their trailer had a bird's-eye view of the church. My grandma wandered the compound daily, and if she saw more than one car pull up to the church, she would rush and gather all the children (my four cousins and my sister and me) and tell us, "Hurry up and get down there. Something's going on at the church." We would run and join in on the festivities, even weddings of people we didn't know.

As an adult, a boyfriend's parents told me they were married in that same church many years ago. My boyfriend was about six years old when they married. They were skeptical when I told them I was probably at their wedding. They pulled out their photo album, and sure enough, there was the girl with the messy white hair and a rainbow sundress. The craziest part is that I was sitting just a few feet away from their son, whom I would eventually meet over twenty years later.

So, yes, I am certifiably Christian. But back then, I didn't know it was my religion; I thought it was my nationality. Someone once asked me where I came from, and I responded, "Christian." I was very believable. I don't recall any feelings of awkwardness.

My grandparents had a mean cat named Polly Carp. She was black with long claws and shiny, knobby, matted fur. She must have been one hundred years old. She would attack if anyone tried to pet her. We would try "for sport" to see who would get attacked. My grandma would rough Polly Carp up until she would attack her. The cat would claw my grandma's hands, but she would never cry. I believed her hands were made of leather. Fresh scratch marks lined her hands and arms so much it was difficult to see the wounds that had healed. Grandma said the old broad was tough, but not as tough as her.

My grandma was gentle but firm. She wore shapeless house dresses and white socks up to her knees, with white nurse-style shoes. Her legs were pudgy like a baby's, with rolls in them, but her skin didn't look new. She had short, gray hair and wrinkly skin with brown marks all over. She also wore thick, small-sized eyeglasses. Our entire family admired her. She was famous for her "potato dumpling" recipe, which she often made for birthday celebrations. This dish was always a big hit with everyone.

My grandma randomly walked around the compound and usually ended up at our trailer. If I was too hyper, she sat on me. I would try to wiggle to get her to let me up, but I would just have to give up. She was a little on the chubby side; she was too heavy to escape out from under. Since I couldn't escape, I had to talk to her. We always talked about church. She told me all about the Bible, too. In fact, she shared wisdom with me when I was seven, which would save my life twelve years later. "Jenny, if you ever need help, pray to God. He will help you."

Every night, I prayed. "God, please help me. Please teach my mom to be nice. Please make my dad happy. Please help Jay Jay be normal again. Also, God, please make me the best storyteller ever, so people will finally listen to me."

God didn't think I needed help because nothing ever changed. I continued to pray, though.

My grandpa was sweet too, but a man of few words, like my dad. He liked to drink buttermilk, listen to Christian music, and work on things around the compound all day. You could easily find him underneath the hood of one of the many clunkers parked near his trailer. He wore motor oil like it was skin lotion—unless he was going to church, then he would wash up and put on a suit. He said we all had to look nice in the house of God. I dreaded seeing him pull out his black pocket comb around me because I knew he planned to use it on my white, tangled hair. He was always careful, but I would cry the entire time. The more I fought it, the longer it took, he said. So, I tried to stay put. When he was finished, I would rush to the bathroom mirror and admire my new pretty hair.

His fingernails were thick and black for some reason, but he said they didn't hurt. He was thin, and he didn't have much brown hair. He seemed to be part Norwegian and part turtle because he would drive so dang slow! He would hum and scratch his head with his beetle-looking fingernails. When he drove, he never even turned around to speak to me; he kept his eyes on the road.

"You must always drive with caution," he would say.

"Why?" I knew the answer, but he couldn't see the devious smile on my face.

"Safety, Jenny. People's lives are on the line."

When someone drove too fast, he would growl the word *criminy*. My eyebrows would raise and my lips would purse as I tried to hold in my laughter.

Ironically, he would die some years later in a car accident that involved a speeding driver.

My grandparents were nice to have around. They helped out with my brother sometimes. When my grandma was nearby, my mom was kinder. I thought things might be getting better, but I soon found out that wasn't the case.

When I was seven years old, I would get my third job, the hardest task yet. My mom told me she had to talk to me and brought me into a room and made me look at her uncertain eyes.

"I'm going to give you the most important job of your life."

My heart sank, and a sense of impending doom leased a hold on me. I knew this new form of punishment would be harsh. Yet I acted undismayed and asked, "What is it?"

"It is your job to make sure Jay Jay doesn't get away. If he does and he dies, it will be your fault, and everyone will blame you."

My Dad, Jay Jay, and Janna

Love, Hate, and the Hollow State

"Many abused children cling to the hope that growing up will bring escape and freedom. But the personality formed in the environment of coercive control is not well adapted to adult life. The survivor is left with fundamental problems in basic trust, autonomy, and initiative. She approaches the task of early adulthood—establishing independence and intimacy—burdened by major impairments in self-care, in cognition, and in memory, in identity, and in the capacity to form stable relationships. She is still a prisoner of her childhood; attempting to create a new life, she reencounters the trauma."[1]

—Judith Lewis Herman

The treehouse now has a deck on top. I built the deck with my own two hands and with no help. It looks beautiful. I am proud of this accomplishment because I am an Aries. I usually begin projects, do the hard parts, and quit when the challenge is over because I know others can finish the easy stuff. I am inside the treehouse now because it is too cold to write on "The Deck" tonight. That is what I named it: "The Deck." Long planters encase the sides, so I won't easily fall over. One of them has "The Deck" spelled out in nails and screws instead of anything normal, of course. The planters are full of dirt and manure and anything else soft and brown I could find to shove in them. The plants are green because the deck is red, and they shouldn't match. One plant is a tiny rose bush with purple flowers the man in the house

---

1 Judith Lewis Herman, *Trauma and Recovery* (New York: Basic Books, 2015), p. 110

gave me for Valentine's Day. I planted the bush with the new plants on the deck because it looked like it wanted to die.

I'm drinking a smooth white wine that is unfixed and unfiltered. It doesn't give me headaches. Something about dairy gives me horrible headaches, and I did some research and found out milk is in wine.

The other day, I picked up a medical marijuana card. That was a new experience. The pharmacy I went to was serene and clean. I chose some topical pain relievers, some anxiety liquid drops, and three grams of three different strains of marijuana. Is it acceptable to say "marijuana"? I have no clue what is politically correct anymore.

The different flower strains are foreign to me. After smoking the first one, I cleaned the entire garage and was creative as well. As I moved a tall dresser, it fell apart on me. The drawers were still useful, so I drilled them into the wall, and now I have shelves. That is not a task I would typically do, but it was an excellent idea.

The second strain was different. After smoking it, my body was in "Jell-O Land." My body felt heavier than usual. I had planned to try it, fold some laundry, and pack for my upcoming trip to New York. But it was hard to hold my head up. I brought the laundry to the room in the Big House and folded clothes as I sat on the bed watching Netflix. The show *Shameless* popped up on my screen, and I decided to give it a try. Not long after, I was hooked on the show. I watched six episodes. I believe this is called binge-watching, which I never do. As I ate gluten-free pasta with chunky red sauce, I balanced a coconut milk, chocolate ice-cream cone in my left hand. My right hand folded the laundry in strange ways as I stared at the television. The chocolate ice cream would drip onto the clean laundry if neglected for too long. Occasionally, I realized my bottom jaw was dropped open. My mouth is never open when I watch TV.

Tonight, I'm not trying the third strain—better save that one for a special occasion. I'll smoke the first one instead. Smoke fills the treehouse as I focus on the laptop screen. I think of how I dread giving life to this chapter. I'm listening to John Mayer's "Stop This Train," but this is a train I cannot stop.

YOU WOULD THINK I'D REMEMBER every detail of every little thing from my past. To be honest with you, I don't. The birth of my little sister was completely forgotten. I don't even remember my mom being pregnant. I cannot recall any talk of a baby coming or of a baby being born. The other morning, I was brushing my teeth, and my younger sister sent me a text. I texted her back, set my phone down, continued to brush my teeth, and then yelled, "Shit!" So, there you have it. My mom got pregnant and had a baby girl. Now, chronologically in this book, she is two years old.

I found it odd that I didn't remember this, so I asked my dad about the pregnancy. It all makes sense now. He told me they were not trying to get pregnant because my brother was sick. Once my mom became pregnant, the doctor told her the baby was likely to have developmental delays, like my brother. So my mom did not celebrate or tell many people. I did not know she was pregnant. I probably thought she was just fat in the stomach.

My brother now attended school, and a miniature yellow school bus drove all the way up the bumpy gravel road to the compound to get him. Jay Jay would jump, punch the air, and squawk with excitement when the bus pulled up. Gina and I never understood why he went to school when it seemed to us that he was unteachable. My mom said it didn't matter if he learned or not because she now had a free babysitter, and she could breathe a little.

When my brother was not at school, I was his caretaker. At first, it was fun. He would run the other way as I cleverly beat him to every door and window he tried to escape from. Jay Jay was fast. His mission was to break out of the house. He was not allowed out, and I was on "guard duty" all the time. After a few days on the job, I was sick of the responsibility. I wanted to play with my cousins or by myself. Eventually, I became tired of the constant pursuit and tied a rope around his waist to keep him near. Furniture and other inanimate objects held him close so I could do normal activities with the other kids. When he learned of his strength, he began to drag the items he was attached to, or he would destroy whatever was around him as he thrashed to break away.

One day, I was left alone to watch Jay Jay. I barricaded every door and made sure every window was secure. I pretended to be an average child and went into my room to get something. But I was sidetracked and began to draw on a piece of paper. This was a moment of happiness. I stayed in the room drawing, even after I thought the house sounded too silent. The next time I thought about how quiet the house was, I decided to check.

As I walked toward the living room, my heart dropped; I saw sunlight crossing the floor ahead of me. I knew what that meant. As I rushed into the room, I looked to the left in a panic. The door was open, my barricade destroyed. My head filled with curse words. (I knew some by now.) My eyes were bulging, and my hands were shaking. I ran toward the corner of the trailer to see the road beneath. Since the front of our trailer faced away from civilization and toward the mountains, I had to go fast. Right as I rounded the corner, I heard a car. My mom pulled up in the Mazda station wagon. My heart dropped. Then I did a double take and saw my brother sitting in the backseat.

I laughed; I thought it was funny that he ran right into her. My mom, on the other hand, was not happy. She brought my sister and brother into the house and grabbed the fly swatter. I was confused but at the same time terrified by the look on her face. I had stopped laughing by now and tried to explain, but she just started coming after me. I was in disbelief. My mom had come unglued. She cornered me on my twin-size bed and swatted me with the fly swatter on my arms, legs, and anyplace I couldn't cover. I hid my face. I felt the worst fear of my life. I was horror-stricken. She used all of her strength with each swat until she finally lost her breath. Then she left the room.

I sat up and scooted back into the corner as far as I could. I looked at all the marks on my body. Everywhere I looked, they were there. I became angry and slammed my back and head into the corner and started to cry. I was hollow. I felt sadness, guilt, shame, anxiety, worry, and fear. There is one other emotion I felt that scared me the most—hate. I felt hate. I thought she hated me. I thought I hated her. I knew I hated myself. My existence caused me too much pain.

I decided to pray: "Dear God, if you can hear me, please make my brother better or please make my mom die or please make me die because tomorrow is picture day, and I know I will be forced to go to school like this." I crammed myself into the fetal position in the corner and stared at my hands and thought about life. I had to pee badly but held it. I smelled food cooking but was not going to leave that room. I wanted to pray and feel safe.

How could a mother do something like this? Upon further research, I believe this incident was due to family stress and emotional health. The other explanations I had to choose from were of no relevance, considering my mom had a proper upbringing without abuse, did not do drugs or drink, and had a good family support system.

I questioned everything I knew about life in my partially-developed brain. Why did some kids act happy at school? Why did some kids have immaculate clothes and so many of them? Why did some kids have cute lunch boxes and cool lunches? Why did some kids have lovely hair and parents who would kiss them when they dropped them off at school? Why was I different? What did I do to be different? Why did I have to go to the office to explain why I had no lunch? Why did I beg kids for their coleslaw when they were about to toss it off their trays, only to have them laugh at me after giving it to me? Why was my hair thin and ugly? Why did I have the ugliest legs with white spots all over them? Why was my name Jenny? Why couldn't I see the words on the chalkboard at school? Why was I too afraid to tell the teachers I couldn't see well? Why couldn't I read? Why did I pee the bed? Why was I shy? Why did I stare? Why would no one listen to me? Why was I alive? I had no answers for any of these questions and hoped I would die in my sleep. Thus far, this had been the worst day of my life. And it wasn't even over yet.

IN THE MIDDLE OF THE night, the door crept open. I didn't peek to see who it was; I was too scared. I pretended to be asleep. The person sat on my bed. I held my breath; I heard a sigh. My body tensed up. I still pretended to be asleep. Then I heard my mom say the most beautiful words I had ever heard her say in my life: "I love you." She didn't touch me. She just said, "I love you." After a moment, she stood and quietly closed the door as she left. Tears started to roll down my face. I didn't move because I wasn't sure if she would come back into my room. I curled into a ball and wept. I was now sure this was the best day of my life.

I prayed to God again: "Dear God, please don't make my mom die. She is being nicer. And thank you for having her say what she said to me. Also, I don't want to die anymore."

I fell asleep for a while, only to be woken up by a wet bed. I didn't mind peeing the bed because when I did, I would gather up my wet sheets, put them in the dryer with my clothes, and wear a towel. I would lean up against the dryer and pretend it was like a mom. I liked the warmth and the sound of the machine. I felt safe, at times, as I leaned on the dryer. Oddly enough, the dryer was in the kitchen, and no one ever bothered me while I was there. I don't know if they even saw me there. I never saw anyone, but I was usually sleeping.

It was awkward to see my mom the next day. I didn't want to look at her eyes. I was still scared. I wore a long-sleeved shirt and pants underneath the dress I wanted to wear for the pictures. At school, I was called into the office. I don't remember what the principal asked me, but it had to do with my parents hurting me. I automatically said, "No." I felt like it wouldn't happen again, so I didn't want my mom to go to jail. I also didn't know what would happen to me. I think I was mainly ashamed, worried everyone would find out. I just kept saying everything was fine. They let me go, and they never called me into the office again, and I didn't mention the incident to anyone at home.

I DIDN'T HAVE MANY FRIENDS. I usually chose to play with the kids no one liked, the ones others teased and taunted. I was certain these kids wouldn't say no because they had no friends of their own. I had one friend in Sky Valley. I stayed the night at her house once. It was stinky and dirty. Besides that, I played with my cousins at the compound. We had a great time together. We wandered into the canyons where it was fun to escape from the adults.

I had one cousin who seemed rich, and I always burst with excitement when I visited her house in Los Angeles. Her name was Julie. She was an only child and seemed so different from the rest of us. She was a few years younger than I was. She had beautiful, curly red hair and large, doll-like brown eyes and porcelain skin. Everything about her was perfect.

Her closet overflowed with cute new clothes, and I was sometimes allowed to wear them. I felt wealthy and beautiful. She also had all the new toys you would see on commercials. We played house and made potions. She had a perfume-making kit. I loved to make perfume because she let me take what I made home. When I was sad or lonely, I would close my eyes and sniff the sweet perfume and feel hope for the future.

I wanted to be like Julie. She was very nice. We were like best friends. We bonded instantly every time she would visit, no matter how much time had passed.

Julie received a lot of attention. No one seemed to notice me, so I liked the attention she was given. Emotionally, I fed off the tender loving care her parents gave her because it was a rarity for me to see adults treat a child with such kindness.

Julie and I were movie stars. We rehearsed together and put on little shows. Everyone would watch if Julie was involved.

I felt like a princess when I was around her. I even imagined having a daughter one day. I thought about how I would make sure she had lovely things to play with and movies to watch that would not make her feel scared.

When it came time for me to go home, I always asked Julie if I could have some of her stuff. "Don't throw any of your things in the trash ever!" I told her. "Save them for me." I only said this because I occasionally found whimsical little treasures in her garbage. Pieces of broken toys could no longer perform in her world, but they could be the center of attention in mine.

Once, when her mom dropped me off at home, she said, "Jenny, if you want to keep coming over, you have got to stop asking Julie for all of her stuff." As I walked away, I thought about acting like I'd forgotten she had said that the next time I visited.

LIFE WASN'T ALWAYS BAD. Early in the morning, my dad would open our trailer window and yell, "Good morning!" to everyone using a microphone with a super-loud speaker connected to it. We watched *The Jetsons* and *The Flintstones*. My dad enjoyed cartoons. When he was around, I could be a child because there were two adults to watch Jay Jay.

We also learned how to barricade the doors and rig a window like a drive-through. My cousins would cruise up in their invisible cars and order fake food from me. That way, I could watch my brother inside and play at the same time.

Jay Jay took off a few more times while we lived in Sky Valley. Lucky for me, his escaping escapades didn't happen on my watch.

One day, my grandpa came home with a Sit-N-Spin. Jay Jay sat and spun for hours. I felt dizzy watching him, but at least he wouldn't run when he climbed off because he would be falling all over the place.

Gina and I continued to go to church with our cousins, but my parents no longer attended because they were told my brother was disruptive. My mom told us God cursed her. That was the first time I thought she was crazy. The second time was when we were all going to the store. My older sister and I began to fight in the backseat, and my mom pulled the car over and yelled for me to get out. She told *me* to get out—on a long, paved road surrounded by dirt roads in the middle of nowhere. I continued to sit in the car, but she started yelling at me to get out, so I did. I stood between the car and the door, and she said, "Hopefully somebody else will take you, since you can't behave yourself." Then she peeled away. I knew then that my mom didn't like me.

I didn't cry. The anticipated fear of being left on my own suddenly turned into hope. Maybe a kind stranger would swipe me up and offer me an exceptional life. I stood there for a while, kicked the dirt, and waited to be whisked away. When no one came, I began to walk along the lonely asphalt road back toward home. Cars passed; no one stopped.

About an hour later, my mom pulled alongside me with her window down and asked, "Are you gonna behave? Get in!" For a second, I just stood there. Dread filled my blood and made me feel heavy. She would have chased me with the car if I tried to run, so I chose not to. Reluctantly, I climbed into the back and stared out the window and wished I could be somewhere else with other people. The view of her eyes watching me in the rearview mirror made me want to jump out of the car. That was the first time I had thought of death as an escape.

WE DIDN'T STAY IN SKY Valley long. When second grade ended, my report card said I failed and would be held back because I couldn't read well and never participated. My mom didn't even get upset, though I could never really tell because she always spoke to me with venom on her breath. Like a pit bull about to fight a chihuahua, she savored her position of power. She glared at me from behind her thick, tortoiseshell glasses. "You are lucky people think you're cute, or you would go nowhere in life."

She told me that some kids were just slow. And she reminded me that I might have brain damage from when I was dropped on my head as a toddler. She frequently said I was a *numbskull*, so I figured the hospital reports showed that my skull was numb from the incident. Come to think of it, she never called me by my name. *Nitwit* and *twit* were often used to get my attention. I felt angry when she called me *nincompoop* because it had the word *poop* in it. *Imbecile* was also the name of a medicine, but it didn't bother me. The funniest nickname she gave me was *dingbat*, which I didn't mind because I thought bats were cool. She often suggested that I was dumb.

My mom didn't know I had white spots all over my legs. She was not informed, for obvious reasons. To avoid negative attention, I wore pants or pulled my socks up to my knees when I wore dresses. I went to great lengths to hide my vitiligo. God forbid anyone saw my spots, or I would be considered ugly, and I would go nowhere in life.

One day, two big-rig trucks pulled up to our trailer; the trucks had huge boxes on the back. I thought the drivers were lost. The entire compound community gathered around, wondering what this was. Then my dad said, "That's our new house." It was a Geodesic Dome Kit in boxes! He told us he was going to show the guys where to deliver the boxes because he wasn't building his new house in the compound.

We were confused, but when my dad returned, he explained how he planned to build our house in a small town a few miles north. When the weekend arrived, he drove us to see the location. I don't know why I ever imagined something normal. This new spot was far from normal. I thought we lived in the middle of nowhere in Sky Valley, but at least we had electricity. Now, we were literally making our own road by driving over some trail. I wondered when we were going to stop. We were not near any houses. There were no electric poles. It was desert, just dirt and bushes. We finally stopped about a mile from civilization. A tractor parked nearby, nothing else—no water, not one single thing. There was a large, cleared area with two gigantic boxes. My dad got out of the car and said, "Welcome home!"

CHAPTER SEVEN

Where the Grass Is Greener

They say the grass is greener on the other side, and it was because all we had was dirt. We had no house, no water. But I suppose no grass is better than dead grass.

Our minds tell us that where the grass is greener, life is happier, that problems and troubles do not exist. People always smile and laugh; life is better where the grass is lush. My mind tricked me as yours did you. Envy and deprivation brewed inside me. To have less meant any happiness was impossible to grasp. Wherever this place with more was, I wanted to be there someday. And one day when I found it somewhere else, I'd see for myself that it was all true. Once I arrived to the other side, I would look back and see where I came from, and feel appreciation.

The moral of my thought is this: Make do with what you have, even if all you have is dirt and rocks. Maybe your dirt is better than their dirt, and maybe your rocks are stronger than the rocks where the grass is greener. Or better yet, perhaps where the grass is greener, dirt and rocks do not exist.

One week later, we drove again on that bumpy road in the middle of nowhere. The dirt road was long and dusty, a one-way road too narrow for cars to pass each other, probably because it wasn't officially a road yet. It was more like a wide trail people used to hike up the mountain. There was also horse poop on it, hence a horse trail.

We were out about a mile from civilization. My dad seemed to be excited. He told us that we had our own mountain, and a house on the hill would enable us to see Jay Jay if he ran away. Our plot was surrounded by land owned by the Bureau of Land Management (BLM). No one was allowed to build on BLM land, my dad said. We would have privacy and wouldn't have to worry about nosey neighbors butting into our business. He was very happy about that. My feelings were just the opposite. I was already emotionally detached from society. Now I would be physically separated as well.

We drove up the mountain to our destination. There was a large, circular lot ready to build on, and two huge boxes that contained our yet-to-be house inside. I stared at the boxes and wondered what kind of future they held. I was quiet. I didn't feel optimistic, so I tried to use my imagination. One thing I disliked about using imagination was sometimes too much reality would put a halt to it. The truth of some situations would settle in my mind, or I wouldn't be creative enough because I lacked knowledge and experience. I tried to see if there was anything to get excited about, but I couldn't because my eyes were taking in and trying to process what was real.

My eyes were blank as was my mind, but there was something across the valley I could not stop looking at, no matter how hard I tried. The view lit up my soul and saddened my heart at the same time. I was intrigued.

I couldn't see with my imagination, like I usually did. I couldn't create a fantasy world for escape. I could only see reality as it was, and the reality was dirt. Dirt was everywhere, with bushes and hills. We stood there, as if we had been dropped off in the middle of nowhere and were told to start from scratch. I felt naked and empty. I never had many material things, but what little I no longer had was sorely missed and much appreciated.

The noon sun shined high in the sky. Our station wagon sat on the dirt lot with all the doors opened. I stood and held a shopping bag with my entire life inside. My mom was busy with my brother in the car, and my little sister, Janna, amused herself with an exploration of the land. My older sister, Gina, had already disappeared. She was very independent. She probably set up camp somewhere on the mountain, or had an escape car waiting to take her away.

Confusion and disappointment shown on my face. I stared at the lot with my lips sealed and my teeth clenched together, tightly. I didn't blink until dirt finally blew into my eyes.

My dad examined the boxes. At times, he made various sounds that must have represented internal thoughts.

With a shock-induced nervous stutter, I asked, "Where is the water?"

He laughed. "There is no water."

His nonchalant attitude did not amuse me. I was worried we might die. In my mind, we were about to attempt a feat no one else had ever tried or succeeded at, something dangerous and stupid.

Then, as if it was not a problem to him at all, he said, "We will have to find a place in town to fill up some jugs with water."

Dread started to overwhelm my mind as I stood in silence. I thought of another question. I cleared my throat. "What about baths?"

"There will be no baths."

My head tilted with sadness. My eyes widened, and my lips began to quiver. I didn't argue, and I couldn't because we never disagreed with my dad. It had been hard enough to gain the courage to ask him about the water. We respected my dad and even became nervous when we spoke to him. He didn't speak unless necessary. He wasn't mean, but he was intimidating.

There was a flashlight packed in the car. When I saw it, I knew we wouldn't have electricity, at least not for some time. There would be no lights to illuminate the darkness as we slept in the middle of nowhere.

"Girls," my dad said as he pulled the flashlight out of the car. "This belongs to me. The flashlight is not to be used for play. Understand? We will only use this for emergencies."

"What about at night?" I asked him.

"Everything we need to do will be done during daylight. That is all there is to it."

It was hard to comprehend that we would live there, for now, with no water and no electricity.

IT WAS SUMMER, AND THIS mountain was our home. This might sound fun or adventurous to the avid nature enthusiast. But I had no bonds with anyone, not even in my own family. My dad was always focused on work and survival. My mom's attention never left my brother. My little sister was just a toddler, and my older sister was a loner, never to be found. I was alone in my family.

We slept in the car or on the mountain for about two weeks, until my dad had a double-wide trailer brought up from the compound. Our long, white, battered house on wheels had no water or electricity. I had believed the arrival of the trailer meant we would have water and electricity. I was wrong. It meant "shelter" and nothing else.

This might sound horrible to you thus far, but as a child and with the passing of time, living in the middle of nowhere, without water and electricity and a roof over my head, was not awful. Have you ever imagined something in your mind and believed it so much that for those few seconds, you were filled with an amazing feeling? My imagination was my source of happiness, my source of comfort. You could even say my imagination was the key to my sanity.

I taught myself to create things that were not there. I taught myself to change the circumstances inside my head. I began to daydream often. My thoughts made me happy, and I had something to focus on that intrigued me immensely during my waking hours. My imagination gave me hope.

My dad moved quickly and started to build our house. We pretended to be normal. Our food came from boxes and cans, nothing ever hot. My mom would bring home a shopping bag full of surprise canned foods. None of them had labels, just prices written in a black marker. The fifty-cent ones were the best—they usually contained beans or corn. Gina and I would fight over them. No one ever wanted the ten-cent cans; they were banged up and usually contained something gross in them.

Our water came from a spout on the back of the local convenience store. We hauled empty jugs and filled them up. My mom would pull right up behind the store, with no shame. If I ever saw a kid my age or older, I would hide. I was embarrassed, but once the jugs were full, I was happy to have water. When we returned home, I always hid a jug behind a rock on the mountain, for my personal use. I hated feeling dirty, so I cleaned myself with the water. No one ever knew.

Soon after our move to the mountain, we set up lookout points for spotting my brother. My brother would try to run away but wouldn't get far because we always saw him. There was nowhere to hide. It was still my job to watch him. But I grew tired of chasing him. One day, I found a rope and tied it around his waist. He had so much energy and strength. If he ran, he would pull me, so I soon realized I had to tie him to unmovable objects like cars or trees. I sat near him while he tried to break free. I talked to him as if he could understand me. I tried to pretend to be a "normal" child, but I had forgotten what normal was.

My brother and I developed a bond. He was someone I could talk to. But he was like a hyena disguised in a human body, only capable of moving fast and making strange noises. I spent most of the day with him and often prayed for God to fix him. I felt certain that if he was normal, everything else could be normal too.

From the first day on the mountain, I imagined living where the grass was greener. We had no grass, only dirt, but there was a place that was normal, a place not in my imagination. Every day, I would mentally go to this place as I was physically dragged around the mountain by my brother on a rope.

The mountain adjacent to ours boasted life: families, children, birds, trees, and grass. Civilization. This was the place I could not take my eyes off of. Imagine a vast, C-shaped mountain. We lived on the south side of the C, and they lived on the north side. Desert wildlife lived in the middle. There were also desert washes. But there were absolutely no homes. There was so much rugged desert in the middle you couldn't even walk across to the other side. It divided us from civilization. We were separated from them; we were not a part of their community. We knew no one, and no one knew us. Division gives you a sense of difference, and different we were.

We had binoculars in case my brother got away. I used them to stare at the other side for hours. Sometimes my eye sockets would hurt, or I would get a headache, but the pain never deterred me from my guilty watchful pleasure.

In my mind, I helped people carry in their groceries and put them away. The neighborhood children played with me. I had my own tree-house. Barbecues and music were a regular part of my days. I had a room with a TV and lights that shut off at the same time every night. There was a beautiful bed for me, with someone to tuck me in and kiss me goodnight.

When I traveled emotionally to the other side, I was normal. I had families and friends who did not know they had me. I lived to watch others live.

While I write this, I smile. I let the nostalgia of my childhood "self-pity" bring comfort. I am now "where the grass is greener," and the experience of looking back to a time when the grass seemed impossibly far away is, well, it's just magical. Magical in a sense that I get to relive all the emotions, all of the depths of humanity I experienced, and still know that when the show is over, I can return home. As ironic as it seems to find comfort in revisiting a place and time where there was none, it is true. Turning back the clock always gives me a sense of joy.

By the time the summer of 1981 was about to end, my dad had the entire frame of the house built. There was no roof yet, just beams, two-by-fours, and splintery wood flooring upstairs and on the stairs. The bones of the house were in place. The entire process of the house coming to life was surprising and thrilling.

First, there was a huge round slab of concrete for flooring. We could play hopscotch, bounce balls, and pretend to ice skate under the stars at night. The frame was built on this slab, of course. There was wood everywhere, and a large scaffold that brought hours of entertainment.

The experience of the transformation—from two huge boxes to a framed, two-story house—was more than magical; sometimes I did not know if it was reality or my imagination. I was not impressed with the fact that ours was a unique home because I did not yet know the difference between ordinary and extraordinary.

I slept in an open-roofed house with a fantastic view of God's starry sky. I had a small room upstairs. Gina claimed the large one.

Because the house was round, the roof was curved, thus making the outer walls curved. Some of the bedroom walls were straight up and down, but because the roof was bent, the walls did not touch the ceiling. There was about a four-foot gap between the bedroom walls and the ceiling. A hammock made out of a sheet hung between two four-by-fours. Material from my grandma made beautiful walls.

The less you have, the more creative you become. When you are always forced to think outside the box to create a sense of normality, it becomes a life skill. The process is complicated but satisfying, at the time.

When you eventually have more to work with, the talent stays with you, and you naturally approach things differently than others. Solutions that seem reasonable to you seem unique and creative to others.

My responsibilities ceased at night. My brother slept with my parents wherever they slept. Fantasies controlled my mind at dusk. No cares were present, and the vast night sky transformed into a magical movie screen. The feelings I could create in my soul were out of this world. Someday, I knew these feelings would become real, and I would be set free.

I found solace in strange places: the expansive night sky, the mountain where the grass was greener, and inside the two-seater outhouse.

My dad built a two-seater outhouse in case two people had to go to the bathroom at once. There was never anyone else in there when I used the outhouse, though. If the door was closed, I used a bush instead. The outhouse was nice … for an outdoor bathroom. A toilet paper roll and a magazine rack were on each side. The outhouse brought comfort during the day. If I had to use it, I could relieve myself from responsibility and lock myself away from reality for five or ten minutes and look at magazines. The only thing I hated was that it smelled like crap.

IN ORDER TO NAVIGATE THE house at night, I memorized every square foot of the rooms and hallways. This feat was accomplished through persistent practice sessions: I walked the path again and again with my eyes shut during the day. Like many lessons, I first learned the importance of the need for this skill the hard way. One night, I attempted to go downstairs to the outhouse and reached out to the railing to stabilize myself. There was no railing; I fell far. Night struggles like those led to some great innovation. I soon created a duct tape trail from my room, down the stairs, through the living room, and to the front door. I would walk along that trail like it was a tightrope, with arms out to make sure nothing was in the way. The success of the duct tape system was extremely gratifying.

You can have a lot of fun inside an unfinished house. Missing drywall, open floors, exposed rafters: all of these served to make our half-finished house my circus. I could climb the walls and tie my brother to the exposed studs. Hide-and-seek at night was a blast. I mastered the feat of balancing myself on top of a sideways fifty-five-gallon drum and rolling my way across the yard. The place was a major hazard, of course, and after an imperfect jump one day, a warped beam landed on my toe. The result of my blunder was a blackened toenail that fell off shortly after.

I began to see the possibilities of what the house could become, and what that could mean. Life started to look better to me.

My mom began to read a favorite tabloid magazine to us for entertainment. It had all kinds of freaky and bizarre stories she said were true.

"This woman had a two-headed baby." She turned the magazine to show us.

My eyes widened. "I guess she was cursed too."

My mom's excitement lessened. "Poor woman."

When Mom was nice, I liked her so much. She seemed like she was a different person.

She still yelled and screamed and hit me now and then—only me, never my siblings. I was the scapegoat. One time, she started to hit me inside the house, so I ran outside to look for my dad for protection. He had failed to protect me in the past, but he had never seen any of the violent assaults. If he were to watch while it happened, maybe he would believe me and help me. I had gone to him for help before, and he reminded me that if my bones were not broken, I was fine.

"If kids behaved in the first place, they wouldn't get hit," he would say.

Now that I was a bit older, I began to rebel and talk back to my mom. Her behavior was wrong, and I wanted it to stop. This time she was furious, and she stalked me inside the house and around the property, occasionally losing her breath because I was fast. She had no fly swatters or belts, but I still felt terror. She reached a point when she couldn't chase me anymore and tried to lure me to her. She stood hunched with her hands on her knees, with a red, puffy face. She struggled to get her words out.

"Come here," she said.

I walked slowly backwards. "No, you're going to hit me."

She tried to stand, then bent back over. "I won't. Come here."

"No," I said. "I'm sorry. I'm sorry. Don't hit me." I tried to sound apologetic so that she would change her mind.

"Here." She stood up. "Let me give you a hug." Her arms reached out.

My eyes squinted, and there was a whine in my voice. "No. You're tricking me."

She huffed and tried to stay standing erect. She took a breath and spoke right through her next words. "I'm not, I promise it's over. Let's hug."

My mind raced as I tried to determine if I should risk an attack for my mother's affection. My arms were crossed with each hand on the opposite shoulder. My chest and heart needed to be protected from her. Cautiously, I walked toward her as I trembled. Then I stopped.

"Promise?" I asked.

"Yes, come on," she replied.

When I reached her, I opened my shaky arms and reluctantly wrapped them around her thick waist. Just as I thought I was safe and imagined my mom loved me after all, I felt like I was being attacked by an animal. She snatched me by the hair and hit me anywhere she could. My face was not off-limits. When she was in a tizzy, she did not care, and she did not punish with love. What she exhibited was hate, pure hate.

"You little bitch." She kept her grasp tight so I couldn't escape her grip. "You think you're better than everyone else."

After breaking free from her clutches, I ran. "You're a bitch," I yelled as I skedaddled over the hill. "I hate you."

When I was far away from her, I sat down on the mountain and anxiously tended to my wounds. My dad was somewhere on the property and surely heard the commotion. *If my mom hurt me harsh enough, he would care and help me, and she wouldn't harm me anymore*, I thought. No bones were broken, but he didn't know that. His shovel aggressively plowed into the earth as I formulated retribution. A rock beside me grabbed my attention. My hand quivered as my fingers folded around it. I clenched it tight in my hand, took a deep breath, squinted my eyes, and smashed it into my face. Blood gushed everywhere. The pain was intense; I was undaunted. After I frantically buried the rock, I ran to the ditch my dad stood in and demanded his attention.

"Dad! Look! Look what Mom did to me!" I said as he turned around. "I think she broke my nose." Blood dripped from my nose onto my hands and shirt.

He took a look at me and was not surprised. "I bet you did it to yourself." He continued to dig.

"No! Mom attacked me! Didn't you hear her?"

He never answered. Gravity assisted the drama as blood splattered onto my nasty bare feet. But it was too late; he had gone back to work as if the last five minutes never happened. Frozen in defeat, I stood there and wished I would bleed to death. Maybe then he would bury me in that precious ditch of his. *It was my fault; it was all my fault*, I thought, after I told myself I was a stupid idiot to think he would have swept me up in his arms and defended me. Disappointment was unearthed in the ditch that day.

There was never any time to bask in my own despair. Self-hate killed me. Reluctant to indulge in my madness, I headed back toward the house. Simple flickers of normalcy would get me back on track, and it just so happened that this night was bath night. Because it only happened once a month, bath night was special.

Baths went in order of seniority, according to my mom. My dad and Jay Jay went first, then her, then Gina, and finally me. The only good thing about the situation was that my mom loathed baths, so she never took them, and she wouldn't give them to my little sister either.

The bathtub was installed before the house was even complete, but the bathroom area was enclosed. Because our bathtub was humongous and our water came from the tank on the top pad, we had to share the same water. That meant by the time I got in, the water was cold and black.

On the evening I smashed the rock into my face, I took my bath, but the dark water did not bother me. By now, we had 9V lights connected throughout the house, generated from the battery in the car. The light was dim, but it didn't matter. As I soaked in the murky water, I found delight in reminiscing about the time our goat, Dolly, got upset, bombarded my mom, and broke her ugly, oversized eyeglasses with her horns. My mom had searched blindly as her hands scoured through the pellet-sized poop and damp hay, in an attempt to locate the popped-out lenses. Her face looked distraught, and her lens-less eyeglasses hung sideways from her pissed-off face. She called Dolly a bitch, over and over. Anytime I needed to feel satisfaction, I'd think of this. It was like Dolly got back at her for all the bad things my mom had done or would do, almost like divine intervention.

When my mom wasn't on a vicious rampage, she was a pleasant person to be around. I began to imagine in my mind that she was two people. *My mom* was the "mean lady" who hated me and wanted me dead, and *Alice* was nice and, sometimes, appeared to have a heart. For some reason, this helped me to differentiate the two.

WE BEGAN TO FIND OUR place on the south mountain. The north began to lose its appeal to me. Our bizarre, spaceship-style home had started to get the attention of the people on the other side, where the grass was greener. People now seemed interested in us and would recognize our cars at the local convenience store and ask my mom questions. My mom would tell them we were building a geodesic dome, and the looks on their faces made me feel that maybe our house was special. My mom was annoyed when people asked questions. She wished they would mind their own damn business, but I liked their inquiries because they seemed fascinated by my dad's creation.

When summer was near its end and school was about to start, my dad told us he had a surprise. His boss gave him two weeks of vacation, and we would head to Oregon on a trip. This was a shock to us because Gina, Jay Jay, and I were set to start school the next week. Gina and I were to attend the same elementary school together, and Jay Jay would attend a special school for children with disabilities. The announcement of this vacation brought both excitement and terror.

The bond between two children begins when school starts. If you arrived late, your opportunity to find companionship was botched, especially if you were introverted like me. Whichever kid was left over, after all the other boys and girls paired up, was the one I planned to befriend. Aggressive kids had more friends, and it was not my nature to compete. Beggars could not be choosers, my mom always said. She usually spoke these words around dinnertime, but I found her wise words to ring true in many situations.

Before we left for Oregon, I hung up a pretty dress my grandma gave me for school, so it would be ready when we returned. My knee-high socks were washed with dish soap in the water behind the convenience store and hung to dry near my dress. These socks were very special to me because they covered all of the vitiligo on my legs. "Cow-Girl" *was not* a name I would be called at my new school.

My school outfit was ready and clean. The other clothes I had were not good enough to wear to school because they were stained or laden with holes. No, this was not my first-day-of-school outfit. This was my one-and-only school outfit. Yes, I was about to go on vacation and start second grade at a new school two weeks late, and I planned to wear the same dress to school every day. Back-to-school shopping was not a ritual my parents chose to take part in.

Fear was an emotion I knew well and was what I felt when I thought about my return to school. An accidental disappearance while on vacation started to appeal to me. *Would it matter if I disappeared?* Life would be a whole lot easier for me if I did not have to explain to others the reality I tried to escape. Only a poor person lives in an incomplete house, without water and electricity. Nobody would ever want to be friends with a girl who lived an uncommon lifestyle like mine.

My grandma once said, "If you can't handle a situation on your own, give it to God." The start of the new school year was the thing I couldn't handle, so I prayed. I prayed for the other kids to like me. I prayed for just one of them to be my friend. If God could just unite me with one other kid who was as lonely as me, be them ugly, dirty, or smelly, I would be eternally grateful. Since I didn't have the self-esteem to be choosy or even to approach another kid, I did what my grandma said and left it to God.

Janna, Jay Jay, me, and Gina

CHAPTER EIGHT

Two Weeks and Twenty-Eight Minutes

Some people have many friends. Some people have one friend.
Some people have no friends. Once upon a time, I had no friends.
But once upon a time never lasts forever.

Being popular and having many friends was something I always fantasized about, but I knew that would never happen for me. I was too socially awkward, and it seemed like too much work, primarily because I was afraid to talk and had no self-esteem or confidence. I have always only wanted just one friend. Through my life, I have had many "best friends." I have traded in old ones for new ones here and there. I'm very difficult to become friends with if I already have a best friend; only the extraordinarily perseverant can take the place of the other friend. Some have tried; some have succeeded. Others have failed or have been traded in for new. I wish I wasn't like this, but I know no other way. One friend at a time is all I can handle, and I would have one at most times.

TWO MONTHS AGO, I FOUND an antique desk at a thrift store. The reddish-brown tint of the desk is speckled with water stains and scratch marks that I know nothing about. It has eight legs, four on each side, to support the three drawers above them. Two of the legs are held on with duct tape because they broke when I moved it.

I'm in the "Big House" because the hot temperature outside is too severe to be in the treehouse today. There is a big window in front of me, with a view of the backyard. There are sheer, white curtains, with white twinkle lights peeking through them, but they are not on. The "Big House" boasts soft touches throughout, created by yours truly. The curtains are closed, but I can see Earth's palette of colors beyond them. Dying roses, in a vase, hold real estate on the left side of the desk, along with a tall, white candlestick holder and a crooked, flaky, never-lit candlestick on top. A faded gold frame holds a postcard painting of a light-skinned, black man with an afro. He has a determined and accomplished look on him, but I have no idea who he is. On the right is a small succulent arrangement, a twine-wrapped, battery-operated vanilla candle, and three pomegranate-colored vintage books: *A Midsummer Night's Dream*, *Hamlet*, and *Antony and Cleopatra*. I created this show.

In the center are my hands and the black keys I push to translate the contents of my mind to you. I wear large earphones; they cover my entire ears. The music is loud. My head randomly sways to-and-fro. The sun shines brightly. I have never written like this before. There is no smoke and no wine. No vices are needed to take this trip back in time.

Two weeks late and going on twenty minutes now. The school year had begun, but this was my first day. Nervous couldn't begin to explain the achy pit I felt in my stomach. My mom always had a way of talking to the Circle K employees about anything and everything. While doing so, time meant nothing to her. The day had begun, and kids came in with their moms or dads and then rushed off to make it to school on time. I noticed their beautiful clothes and became more petrified by their excitement to get to school. That probably meant they had friends. Eventually no more kids were coming into the convenience store.

I stood there, eating a twenty-five-cent Ding Dong for breakfast. I liked to suck the cream out of the center and put my tongue where it used to be. I stared at the back of my mom's head, occasionally speaking in a humdrum voice, "Mom, come on. I'm late." She never listened to me. I cleared my throat and scuffed my shoe on the ground to try and get her attention. It was not until the Circle K employee said, "Oh. She's gotta get to school," that my mom even acknowledged I was there.

I arrived at school two weeks and twenty-eight minutes late. After a stop in the office, I walked to my modular classroom. Imagine a perfectly square classroom made out of wood. It was lifted so high off the ground that a ramp was needed for access. The closer I walked toward the small building, the more I wished the earth would open up and eat me alive.

Nausea overtook me; I felt ready to faint. Physical illness to the point of vomiting would have been welcomed in this situation. It would yield me freedom for being late or even a no-show. I had used the excuse before, but the illness never came naturally. Instead of being brave, I tried to make myself throw up. As I forced myself to burp over and over, I was so on edge that when a classroom door behind me slammed shut, I physically jumped. Cautiously, I crept up the ramp toward my class, staying just below the window so no one would anticipate my arrival.

My mouth felt gross, and I knew I had stinky chocolate breath. As I approached the door, I stopped and looked down at my dress and knee-high socks to make sure they looked acceptable. Like in any horror movie, my hand trembled as I reached for the doorknob. I didn't even manage to turn the knob on that first attempt. Instead, it had been as though I was checking the knob for heat, in case there was a roaring fire on the other side of the door. In a way, there was.

My hand retreated, and I prayed.

Reaching for the knob a second time triggered something like an out-of-body experience. I was coping by displacement so intensely that it briefly felt as though I had gone somewhere else. I wished I could stay there. My eyes squeezed tight, giving me the appearance of an untrained civilian who was trying to defuse a bomb.

Red wire? Or blue?

As the door opened, it seemed as though it was the only thing that was moving. I, along with the school and the rest of the world, seemed suspended in space and time.

The loud voices turned to silence, and I could feel thirty sets of third-grader eyes staring to see who had stepped in through the door. When I walked in, I did not look at them. I saw the teacher's desk in front of me, so I headed straight to it with my head down but my eyes on her. I was uninteresting, and I was undoubtedly not a threat. The kids all began to talk and carry on again as I handed the teacher my note from the office.

My head lifted to look at the class after I was sure they weren't looking at me. When I scanned the room, something caught my eye. A pretty girl smiled and waved at me. She looked like a mix of Laura Ingalls and an angel. I was in disbelief. I questioned if this was my imagination. A confused smile was all I could offer in return.

The teacher assigned me a seat and quieted the class down. She announced that I was new, and everyone chimed, "Hi, Jennifer." I hated the attention and thought it was completely unnecessary. After I settled into my desk, I waited for an opportunity to examine the girl who waved. *What is wrong with her?* I asked myself. Surely no one pretty and normal would be interested in me. Maybe she thought I was someone else. I peered at her. She seemed normal, talking and laughing with the others. She was thin and had long, chestnut brown hair, thick like a horse, not like my thin and stringy hair. She wore a clean dress, knee-high socks, and tennis shoes like me. I examined the rest of the kids to find that we were the only ones with this style. *Why did she have knee-high socks on? Could she possess the same ugly legs as me?*

Now and then, she would notice me staring. The fear of being caught red-handed was instantly disarmed when she actually returned my look with a smile. The positive turn of events threw me into a trance. The feeling was like standing outside in the winter cold, staring through foggy windows that framed the perfect image of some other family sitting around a fireplace, drinking hot cocoa. This was a recurring feeling that happened anytime I beheld friends enjoying each other's company.

In this case, though, I just might have been welcomed inside that cozy home. I forgot where I was and got lost in the thought of where I could be. Involuntarily, my head cocked to the side, confused but delighted. Then came the unexpected sensation of a smile. Not hers, but mine. I even laughed out loud, but stifled it quickly, straightened my head, and stared at the chalkboard. While I outwardly pretended to be an attentive student, on the inside I began to question the imminent future. Positive thoughts were an elusive experience for me, though, and I soon began to think the worst. A slideshow of pre-enactments started to play out in my mind.

The excitement I initially felt when I first noticed the girl diminished as I wondered what I would talk about with her. I couldn't tell her about my living situation, my mom, or my brother. The teacher's voice became the background jumble to my self-deprecating thoughts. *Should I lie? Should I pretend to be rich? I can't be myself; then she won't like me. What happens when she sees me wear the same dress every day? What if she laughs at me?* Just as my internal hyperventilation began, the bell rang. My heart stopped. The students bolted out the door to recess. I jumped up and walked fast. I headed to the restroom to take cover. I would rather avoid everything than face anything potentially harmful to my spirit. I was emotionally fragile and didn't want to cry on my first day. I was nearly tripping over my shoes when I heard a sweet, winded voice from behind me.

"Jenny. Jenny. Wait up."

It was obvious I was in a hurry. In disbelief, I turned as if I didn't know she was talking to me. She was behind a few kids, trying to catch up to me.

"Wait. Don't you remember me?"

I stopped until she caught up.

"From Desert Hot Springs School? I'm Tyler."

So far, the only thing wrong with her was that she had an odd name, but that didn't matter.

She continued as we walked: "I just moved here. I don't know anyone either." This was like Christmas to my ears. I didn't want to speak because I had never heard anything so beautiful.

I heard her speak again. "Jenny, I know you from another school. I know you're poor and sometimes dirty and you're shy. But I have no friends. You are familiar to me. Do you want to be best friends?"

"Yes," I said. There were no other words necessary. I was so happy. I felt like picking her up and spinning her around, but I had to pretend to be normal. We laughed and talked. I still had to act like I needed to use the restroom to justify my speedy exit from the classroom. In the stall, I folded my hands and looked to the sky and mouthed, "Thank you. Thank you." Then I flew out of the bathroom without flushing the toilet or washing my hands, not because I was excited, but because that was not a habit I had grown accustomed to.

We made our way to the playground. Within moments, I was comfortable enough to share the real me with her. Tyler thought I was funny; she laughed at me several times. I loved that. No one ever thought I was funny. She was kind and understanding. I told her the truth about anything she asked. I wasn't ashamed because it was all okay with her. There were times I thought this new friendship might be a dream, and I had to check myself with a pinch. Then I would laugh and look away with a massive smile on my face.

We bonded instantly. We apparently both developed our clothing style from our previous school. I didn't remember Tyler from that school, but I just went along with this thought to have more in common with her. I recognized some of the names of other kids she mentioned to me. I thought I possibly remembered her from the monkey bars. I knew we were not in the same class because I didn't know her name. I couldn't see far; I was nearsighted. That is probably why I only remembered her from the monkey bars, but she remembered me a lot more. On the monkey bars, you see each other up close, but the playground was massive, and I never remembered seeing her there.

I WAS EXCITED TO GO to school with this new friendship to give me hope. Tyler never made fun of me for wearing the same dress to school every day. She didn't care. She continued to wear the knee-high socks with tennis shoes as I did. Maybe she was so nice because she had "Cow-Legs" like mine? I figured I would find out one day, if she ever took her socks off in front of me. Until then, I would wait. I wouldn't want to scare her by showing her my legs. What if she thought my spots were contagious?

One day, the teacher read notes from our parents stating what we were to bring to an upcoming class party. When she got to Tyler's note from home, the teacher said, "Tyler: Yum Yums." The entire class, including myself, burst with laughter. Tyler's mom was supposed to write something specific, like chips or cupcakes, but she wrote "Yum Yums." Tyler's face turned bright red. She was so embarrassed. She looked at me; I tried to keep a straight face. The rest of that day, kids would walk by us and snicker and say, "Yum Yums."

I am laughing so hard right now. The thought of that simple and silly moment has stuck in my mind for over thirty-five years, and it still has the same effect on me. It still packs enough emotion to bring not only laughter, but the tears that are currently rolling down my cheeks. Every time I think of this memory, I lose my composure all over again. I need to try and put myself together, but I keep imagining the look on Tyler's red face. It was as if those words were a complete shock, a mystery that was not revealed until a mind-blowing plot twist. I'm sure her mom got an earful after school that day. I'm also sure that she had never imagined those two simple words would end up finding their way into a book over three decades later.

Tyler and I were inseparable. She invited me to spend the night at her house; I was thrilled. We walked to her home from school. She had no idea how happy I was to have a night away from the mountain. She lived near civilization and the town park. Her home was immaculate and brand-new. The air had a pleasant scent, and the furniture was decorous. Tyler told me her mom furnished the house with her "points" from working at AT&T. *What a fantastic job to have*, I thought. Her bedroom was small but clean. Two cozy twin beds, with colorful comforters that matched, were positioned side by side, about four feet from each other. Tyler was not spoiled by any means, but she did have fun toys and nice stuff. She had ninety-nine percent more than I did. Her large, white closet door was pushed open to one side, as if it welcomed us to enter. Inside, she had Cabbage Patch Kids, Rubik's Cubes, Shrinky Dinks, and all kinds of other cool toys. We pulled out all of the closet's contents, but never touched the cute clothes. We had so much fun that I prayed for time to stand still, but it never did.

Tyler and I went on many adventures together. We would crawl into the large, rusty flood pipe under the highway and listen to the traffic above us. I would often begin conversations with, "What if ..." or "Pretend that ..." Reality was a miserable existence I had learned to escape on my own, but I discovered it was more fun to escape with someone else—someone who encouraged my creativity and imagination, someone like Tyler.

I loved sleepovers at Tyler's. I admired her but never wanted to be her, only because if I was her, I couldn't be friends with her. With Tyler, I could be myself. Happiness filled me, and moments of fun were everywhere. Then, at around seven o'clock in the morning, my mom would show up with blasts from the car horn. My dad was at work, so I had guard duty.

Tyler's dad always seemed a bit grumpy. He would bark at us: "Close the door. Are you trying to cool the whole neighborhood?"

When Tyler got us something to eat, he seemed to monitor everything. Tyler and I learned to avoid him. Tyler's mom was more patient. She was pretty. She wore makeup, skirts, and high heels. She talked softly; she never yelled. I was not used to that. Her mom was loving; I secretly loved that. My mom wore old T-shirts, worn-out stretch pants, and water shoes. My mom did not care if her clothes were dirty, and she sometimes wore mismatched socks. I always thought Tyler's dad and my mom would be perfect for each other.

Her mom would offer gentle reminders for us to "brush those teeth" or "put on jammies." In my house, there were no toothbrushes, and we surely didn't wear "jammies." One of my favorite parts about spending the night was that I got to wear Tyler's pajamas. And yes, I would sneak her toothbrush and use it in order to feel like a regular child, not to be deceitful.

"Normal" was what I often pretended to be. If people saw me in my natural habitat, they would view me differently—like some animal. An animal is not what I wanted to be. *What if Tyler spent the night at my house? Would she ever want to talk to me again?*

Tyler loved adventures. If I invited her over, she would view the lack of water and electricity as highly interesting. She would enjoy our goats, but would give the milk a pass. My maze of duct tape would have her wanting to walk the path from my room to the outhouse with her eyes closed. Even if she found our toilet situation strange, I knew she would love it. I would never know if she thought my home was peculiarly wonderful because I had never invited her over.

Elementary years were enjoyable, but probably not for anyone who got within three feet of me. I barely had any water to clean myself, and no clothes to change into. I always hid one jug of water for a quick wash, but "wash" might be an overstatement. I hardly ever got to clean my hair. It was stringy and greasy.

My dad referred to the rain as a "free shower." Whenever the clouds gathered and the drops started to fall, if the weather wasn't too cold, I would squirt blue dish soap in a cup and find a private spot on the mountain for a proper shower. The rain wasn't exactly dependable, though, and I once ended up with soap in my hair and no water to rinse it out. Still to this day, I have a very special appreciation for the rain.

Dish soap was also used to wash our clothes. We hung them to dry on a sturdy clothesline my dad had built. Every six months or so, we would go to the Laundromat in a nearby town, a real treat for us. Once, I attempted to steal a petite woman's clothes. My sister blocked the view as I put her clothes in our basket. When I began to put the clothes in our car, the lady came outside with a red face and a loud voice, and I had to pretend I didn't know what had happened. I was so embarrassed. I always longed for nice clothes, and they were always worth the risk of trouble.

EVENTUALLY I SAW TYLER'S LEGS, and they were free of vitiligo. When I gained the courage to show her my legs, the white spots were gone, to my surprise! Since I wore knee-high socks all the time, I never noticed when the disappearance occurred. God had answered my prayers and made the spots go away.

When the middle school years arrived, I finally mustered the nerve to invite Tyler to my house. My brother would commit an act toward her that terrified me, and Tyler's reaction would be one I could have never imagined.

CHAPTER NINE

Geodesic Psychedelics

I was in a panic. Objects were thrown into piles and covered with sheets or blankets, a creative and convenient way to make instant couches. This was how we cleaned. My dad had built closets; they were perfect for last-minute decluttering. I cleaned fast when life demanded it.

I felt like I was going to hyperventilate. Tyler had accepted my invitation to spend the night. The few days I gave myself to prepare were not enough. At school, all I could think about was getting home to clean. I didn't want my house to look fancy, just normal. All throughout my childhood, I went to extraordinary lengths to seem normal. I was an actress, famous in Jay Jay's and God's eyes only.

I had been an actress ever since a school trip to a popular movie studio. Not one word was uttered from my mouth the entire trip. The other students' reactions to the actors reminded me of how my parents used to stare at the TV, when we had one. If we made any noise while they watched a show, my mom would turn with angry eyes and place a large crooked finger over her lips. "Shhh! We want to listen to her tell her story."

They would tell us to be quiet because they wanted to pay attention to the little people in the television instead of us. Until our visit to the movie studio, I did not know these people were real. Upon this discovery, I fantasized that I would one day become one of them, someone who captivated the hearts of perfect strangers from different households all over the world. A person who fascinated minds and absorbed attention was the kind of person I ached to be.

The solitude and elevation of my current environment gracefully reminds me that the spotlight is one childhood abstract I do not currently desire at all times. However, I do have an infinite fascination with all aspects of movie production and sets.

When I was young, I heard about a child who purposely got lost at Universal Studios. He was embraced by everyone and later became famous. That child was Steven Spielberg. The difference between Steven and me is that I lost myself for only an hour on our school field trip, but I got scared and found my class. Steven stayed there forever! He basically lived there.

Risk has always been an important aspect of success. For me, trouble came with risk. Steven was braver than I was, and his fearlessness provided me with endless inspiration that I would eventually transform into action.

Many years later, I snuck into Paramount Pictures and immersed myself in the prolific world I was too frightened to explore as a child. There are times when one does not wish to attract attention. My self-guided tour was one of those times.

The entire lot was explored. I saw movie stars but did not recognize them. I walked right onto sets and watched the filming. A spark ignited inside me. I "acted" like I was a movie star, and, apparently, I did a good job. The people in charge began to look for "the lady that paid for the studio tour" but who disappeared from the holding room before it began. I walked tall and smiled at the people who passed by me. I even said hello to some people and waved at the guy on the golf cart who occasionally drove by. I walked through the streets of "New York." It was beautiful. I walked out of "fake stores" and imagined what it would feel like to have all cameras on me while filming a major movie. This was heaven.

Eventually, I grew bored and decided to go back and get on the tour. The guy on the golf cart now had another man with him, a very important-looking man who spoke on a walkie-talkie. When I tried to find my way back, I became even more lost. Finally, I decided to flag the golf cart driver down. I asked him if he could give me a ride to the front. Both men looked confused but agreed to give me the ride. Then I told them I was late for my tour and, before I could finish, they abruptly looked at me and color filled their faces. They were apparently looking for me the entire time, but because my mind is so amazing, I tricked them to believe that I was, indeed, what I pretended to be. They were beating themselves up. "I thought you were … What? Okay. Wait … How?" I just "acted" oblivious to the whole situation, like I was lost.

We returned to the entrance, but the bus had left several hours prior, so I asked for my money back. I had been acting since I was a small child. I acted like everything was normal at home. That takes a lot of skill. It is hard to cover marks on your body and pretend your parents care about you.

I cleaned with haste and shoved all our junk into nooks and crannies. Thank God the house was more standard now. We had a kitchen that functioned and water that ran through pipes to some of our faucets. Our electricity came from the generator and our water from a bus stop spout. Although I was still nervous, I knew we had enough to seem like an ordinary family.

There was a knock at the door and when I opened it, my friend walked in with a huge smile on her face. Everything was going well. But my optimism was destroyed within hours of Tyler's arrival.

I sat on the floor resting my butt on the heels of my feet, hunched over and out of breath. I tried not to cry as I scrubbed as hard as I could. A bottle of Windex sat next to me. I started to mutter a random mix of profanities and my brother's name. As I scrubbed, I began to imagine losing my friend because of what my brother had done. My head filled with questions and thoughts and more questions. *Why? Why would he do this?* Jay Jay had taken a blue ballpoint pen to Tyler's brand-new, white LA Gear shoes—only the most expensive and equally popular shoes around. They had been a Christmas gift. They were still in the box when she showed me.

I knew my brother got into stuff and moved all over the place, but what were the odds of this? *Now what? Is my mom going to come in and hit me?* Tyler probably wondered why I flinched when people reached for things near me. I couldn't help it. I began to pray aloud as the ink started to come off.

After a while, I could hold the shoes away from me and see only white again. The pen marks were gone. There were ballpoint impressions in some areas, but the blue was gone. I took the shoes back to Tyler and hoped she wouldn't see any trace of the disaster. She barely looked as she put them away. She said it was okay. Then she hid them, of course, so Jay Jay wouldn't get them again.

I figured she wouldn't be able to deal with my living conditions without imagination, so I brought her out of my house to explore the property together in safari-like fashion. I told her about the water situation and the generator. The added sense of adventure made the lack of basic utilities seem more exciting than anything else.

We slept on the roof. The air was cold, but that didn't bother us much. We gazed at the sky and talked about everything beneath it.

When the topic of favorite foods came up, I told her mine was pizza. This spawned an epic fantasy that became increasingly real with every word. We imagined a ginormous pepperoni pizza, the size of a UFO, which seemed to manifest itself into reality and come down to the roof. Tyler and I climbed on. We crawled under the pepperoni for warmth and flew away from my house. Beyond the crust of that enormous flying pizza, we saw the world in the form of tiny city lights beneath us. The wind blew through our hair. It was as real as the laughter we failed to contain. When we got hungry, we simply pulled massive amounts of dough up from our soft and warm bed and ate as much as we wanted. It was spectacular. The scenarios we dreamed up were as potent as psychedelic trips.

Surprisingly, my mom didn't butt in often during Tyler's stay. She asked my friend a few questions early the next morning. I tried not to talk to my mom because my voice sounded ugly and because I didn't want to provoke her to hit me right in front of Tyler. Tyler left soon after, which was good because I didn't want her to witness what went on in the dome on the mountain during the day. I didn't know who I was going to get, my mom or Alice. My voice sounded ugly when I talked to my mom because I didn't know how to speak pretty to her anymore. She had said and done so many things to me that my voice changed toward her. I didn't like the sound of it, but I could not change it. I tried many times. Around Tyler, I worked hard to adjust my voice. With Alice, I could speak with kindness, but not with my mom.

Tyler would come over again and again. She liked my house. She loved everything I did to decorate my room. She said I was creative. I thought that was a beautiful word to describe someone who could create necessities that didn't exist.

TYLER REMAINED MY BEST FRIEND year after year, from elementary school through middle school and into high school. School was okay, but it wasn't my favorite thing in the world. Even though I was friends with Tyler, I was still timid. I had anxiety. The report card was never my friend. Terrible grades were marked in most classes because I never had eyeglasses. When I walked, my back was hunched, and I looked at the ground. On the days Tyler didn't show up to school, I would eat lunch in the bathroom stall with my legs up. I was never beaten up in school, so that was one positive aspect.

On certain days of the week, I would walk to my brother's bus stop and get him when my mom couldn't. His little yellow bus had a powerful air conditioner unlike the bus I rode on. He attended regular school but stayed in a special class all day. He could not be left alone because of his fast feet. The rope I carried daily was used to walk him home. Around his waist, it wove through his belt loops and held him tight. These extreme measures insured he would not escape on our long journey home.

One day on the bus, a loud and rebellious teen boy went through my backpack when my attention was elsewhere. He started to badger me and make fun of the yellow rope I had in there. My face became hot with anger. He held it up high and declared that I was a crazy person. He proceeded to make fun of me, while the others whispered and laughed. My eyes filled with tears. Finally, the bus stopped. While I scurried to gather my belongings, I looked out the window and saw my mom preparing to fill the tank on the flatbed truck with water. My heart dropped. As my tormentor began to take notice of her, I grabbed the rope. He yelled out: "Jennifer's mom is stealing water!" I dashed off the bus in shame and embarrassment.

My dad arrived home a few hours later, and I demanded his full attention. The well he had often mentioned would not escape my mind, and I needed answers. He told me that a well is a hole, a bottomless hole. He explained that a tunnel would be dug deep into the ground, and water would eventually be hit. He said the process was costly, and we didn't have the money. Naturally, I began to dig every day after school. While other teenagers did homework, I dug. Dug and dug and dug. A ladder was eventually needed to enter the hole because I dug so much. When I imagined the look on my dad's face after I told him I struck water, I felt proud. My progress would impress him for sure, so I brought him out to show him what I had accomplished. He was genuinely impressed. Then he said, "It is not humanly possible to dig a hole deep enough to strike water." To prove him wrong, I dug a few more days. Then I quit and filled it in.

HIGH SCHOOL GRADUATION WAS AN accomplishment I had no interest in. In twelfth grade, I dropped out of school. When I turned eighteen, Alice and I took classes together to become Certified Nurse Assistants. If we accomplished the course, we would be employed in a house with "crippled" children. Alice said it was a shame anyone would use that word in the name of their business. There were four different houses in one town. The job was excellent for me because of my experience with Jay Jay. And if I saved enough money, I could move off of my parents' property. Alice and I eventually graduated. We were not assigned to the same house because the management didn't want to place family members together for any job position. That rule was fine with me.

Alice drove me to work because I didn't have a car. Although I was technically an adult, I never felt like one. My shyness never dissipated, and I viewed people older than me as authority figures. Like a child, I followed directions and tried to avoid trouble.

This job would change my life forever, in ways I never expected. Never once did I imagine that a position to help people with disabilities would disable me permanently. I had already been through enough bad stuff in life, but I would soon find out my challenges had only just begun.

My dad working on the dome

CHAPTER TEN

Angels with Tiny Heads

When God created the human race, he handed out brains. My mom would tell you I thought he said trains, and I asked for a slow one. If that was indeed the case, I wonder what the children with the shrunken brains believed God had to offer. Because my brain is idle, the pursuit of answers proves difficult. At last, I've come to the conclusion that the size of one's brain does not implicate an abnormality when another one of God's gifts is given to compensate. That gift is the heart.

Bloodcurdling screams came from inside the house on the pitted asphalt road. They were high-pitched. Two girls screamed loudly, and I was the cause of it. Light was scattered throughout the house. We had taken yet another ride in the dark. As the captain of the wheelchair, I turned left and veered right, whenever necessary, to avoid a crash.

They squealed with joy and tried to laugh while catching their breath. I always took them on this adventure. It was ten o'clock at night. It was my shift. I worked alone.

I took care of six girls. Their ages ranged from one to fourteen years. The children were small, and the baby looked like an infant. These girls were familiar. They resembled my brother: innocent and beautiful. This job was second nature to me. My position was to clean the house while the girls slept. Nursing skills and CPR were also part of my training just in case there was an emergency.

The facility I worked at used the word *retarded* in documents to describe the girls. My mom taught us to never call a "special" person retarded because it was not nice and would hurt their feelings. Every time I saw this word at work, I felt uncomfortable. These girls were special.

Two girls were in each of the three rooms. In the first room were two sisters a couple years apart: Linda and Christina. Linda was older. Compared to her sister, she was thin and tall, but she wasn't really tall. She looked tall because she was thin. She was thirteen but looked the size of an eight-year-old girl.

Her sister, Christina, was the opposite—short and round and a ball of absolute joy. She clapped her hands when she saw me and always had a huge smile on her face. She tried to talk but, like her sister, could really only say "no." Linda took longer to say it because she was afraid to open her mouth. Her teeth were always clenched tight, and she walked very stiffly. When I hugged her, she was like a board, with her arms tight and hands in fists by her sides. We encouraged her to drink her nutritional protein drink because she would never eat food. Christina, on the other hand, ate everything in sight. The sisters had microcephaly, and they were special.

In the second room were two girls who were not related: Sasha and Ashley. Sasha had been in an accident when she was little that left her physically and mentally disabled. Her bed had rails, and she had a wheelchair. She always popped her eyeball out, so we had to tape socks on her hands. She was special.

Ashley was one I would watch out for. She was twelve. She liked to rub herself against her bedpost. Then she would grab my arm, and her hands were always wet. It grossed me out. She constantly had her hands in her mouth. She also drooled. I didn't really like human secretions of any kind, so I held my hands up, like I was under arrest, any time she came near. Ashley had microcephaly and was special.

Finally, in the last room, were the little ones: Tess and Violet. Tess was six but was the size of a three-year-old child. She was adorable, with huge blue eyes and soft, curly brown hair. She was like a little monkey; she would climb everywhere and get into things. She had microcephaly and was deaf, and she was special. She understood some sign language, though. She also had a temper, but that just made her more lovable for some reason.

Last was Violet. She was one year old but looked much younger. She would lie on her back in her crib, cooing. She stared at the ceiling while thrashing her arms and legs. She couldn't sit up or crawl or walk. She, too, had microcephaly. She was also blind, deaf, and special.

The kitchen in the house had two sides, one for dairy and one for meat. The dining room had two tables, one pink and one blue. One was for breakfast, the other for lunch and dinner. The girls had strict dietary rules and were only allowed to eat kosher.

Their parents lived in New York and brought them to live here. Only Linda and Christina's parents would ever visit. They came about twice a year, and they sometimes called too. The other children's parents never came or called. Ever.

My life was amazing. I gained my independence and lived in a small trailer on my parents' property. They had water and electricity now, so my trailer had lights. I spent my work money on attractive items to decorate my new home. Since I worked all night, I slept during the day. I used one of my dad's trucks to get to work. It was a big, yellow 1973 Ford. I loved having money and freedom. Alice was nice, and my mom didn't cause a lot of trouble anymore. Occasionally, Alice and I went to the casino and played bingo together. We had a great time. Sometimes I'd say something funny, and she would laugh until she cried. She would beg me to stop. I loved to make people laugh, especially Alice.

I was respected at work, my strong work ethic evident to my peers and manager. Work was my number one priority. I always showed up for work early; I was never late.

Sometimes I took fast food with me. One night, I left my bag in the kitchen and used the bathroom. When I returned, Tess was sitting on the kitchen counter, drinking my strawberry shake, and eating my

French fries. I yelled, "No" and grabbed the food from her. She started to cry, and she was frustrated because she couldn't communicate. I wasn't allowed to let her have outside food because it wasn't kosher. She started biting her arm and pulling her hair. I watched her and thought to myself, *It's not fair that she is like this and has strict rules on top of it.* I knew how happy I always made Jay Jay by adding more fun to his life. I caved and gave Tess the shake and the French fries. I also let her have my extra taco.

After the incident with Tess, I started to incorporate fun things into my nightly routine. If one of the girls woke up to go to the bathroom, they got a ride all through the house in the wheelchair. The real fun came when two of them awoke at the same time. Obviously, I could only push one wheelchair at a time, so they would pile on the same seat for the thrill ride. Each excursion came with a complimentary flashlight for them to shine around in their own light show. The rides concluded with a gentle return to their beds and a kiss goodnight. They didn't have mothers in their lives, so I did my best to fill that role. It was the fulfillment of a fantasy on both ends.

Whenever they woke up while I was doing laundry, it was "Ghost Girl Time." I put a sheet on and chased them throughout the house. Once, Tess conquered her play-fear, rushed me, and pulled the sheet right from my head. She tried to usurp the role of ghost by donning the sheet herself, but ended up running straight into a wall. She was always mimicking, and that time it paid off in laughter tenfold.

One night, as it rained outside, Christina ran into the living room with a tear-streaked face. She was scared of the thunder. I held her on my lap and told her it was okay, but that wasn't quite doing the trick. There's only so much a warm embrace can do in a battle against a larger-than-life monster outside. Surrender was not an option, though. I turned up the radio, opened the French doors to the backyard, ran out, and danced in the rain. She loved it!

The next step was to convince her to come out and join me. She refused, but again, I persisted. After some rummaging, I found her an umbrella. That did the trick. She came out and danced with me. She held my hand, laughing even when the thunder rumbled.

I was in love with encouraging these girls to live their lives to the fullest. I was in love with their laughter, their smiles, and their innocence. My life was perfect when I was in love.

AFTER WORKING AT THE HOUSE for two years, I was informed that I could take a two-week, paid vacation. I was thrilled. At this point, I was earning enough money to get an apartment, so I figured I should search for a place during my vacation. My parents told me I could not use their vehicles if I didn't live next door to them. I didn't care and told them I would ride the bus. I was ecstatic and wanted to get on with life in this beautiful world I was discovering. Each day, I became more confident. I told myself that I was not what happened to me as a child and that I would not fail as my mom had often said I would.

I moved into a small apartment with a friend. The chance to paint my apartment gave me a form of personal expression I had never experienced. Naturally, my artistic sense was intense, and we both agreed pink was the right choice.

My vacation was nice. As bitter as any vacation's end can be, my first one wasn't bad. I was happy, even excited to go back to work. I missed my "babies." Despite my excitement, and partially because I relied on a friend to drive me to work, I was fifteen minutes late to my shift. On the second night, I was thirty minutes late.

The lady at the house warned me that one more slipup would get me reported. Imagine my horror on that third night as I helplessly watched the taillights of my bus zipping past without me. When a kind man offered me a ride, I thought my problem was solved. I never would have imagined that the first stranger ever to be gracious would turn out to be a serial killer.

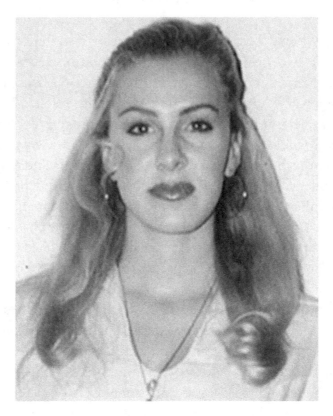

Me at age nineteen

CHAPTER ELEVEN

Talking Telephone Poles

*F*orty-three years post-nativity, while inside my glorious treehouse, I grab a pen and paper and eject some of my often-righteous thoughts. *"Trust is a habit you need to live but a trait that can kill you."* Then my treehouse goes dark.

MY EARS RING. MY EYES expand and feel hot. They begin to bulge out of my head. The car's ceiling looms over me, but I see right through it. The pain from the hands that squeeze my neck is no longer felt.

I am nineteen years old, and I am being strangled to death.

Half an hour ago, I was at the house with the girls. Before I clocked in at work, I missed my bus. After I missed the bus, a nice man offered me a ride. *This must be fate*, I thought. On my way to get into the car, I felt nervous in my gut. I ignored this feeling like I had done all of my life.

The nice man dropped me off at my job and asked for my work number. Fake digits were given, of course. He was not my type, but he was nice. Trust came easy because of his kindness. In my experience, if you acted nice, that meant you were. He was friendly, so I treated him like a friend. We had a typical conversation, and I told him I worked alone at night. He seemed interested, so I told him about the girls under my care. He said he was a detective, hard at work on a dead-end case. We didn't discuss his profession any further because it didn't really spark my interest. He also asked me if I wanted to go to breakfast.

All through the night, I worked without incident. Ten at night until six in the morning. When I left to head to the bus stop in the morning, I heard tires crunching gravel behind me. A light blue Toyota Corolla pulled alongside me, and the man inside smiled. Because I thought he might come back, I was not startled. His persistence was noticed the night before. My preference would have been to never see him again, of course. If I had been bold enough to tell him I was not romantically interested in him, his feelings would have been hurt.

After he pulled up, he told me he was back to take me to breakfast. He seemed happy. After I accepted the ride, we talked casually and joked. Sitting across from him over a meal was not an option in my mind; I only wanted a ride home. He casually asked me about the phone number I gave him the night prior. His interest caught me off guard, but it did not show.

"I guess there was a bit of miscommunication," I suggested.

The mood was calm; I figured he would believe the explanation I offered. Suddenly, he snapped. A rush of horrific energy entered the car. My body became debilitated. My voice was crippled. He exploded with rage.

"You gave me the wrong number! When I called, some old bitch answered."

A gun was held to my temple.

"What? No!" I froze. My breath was absent.

"Shut up, you whore." He became hyperalert to the world around us.

My head was slammed into the dashboard, and I felt a jolt of pain streak through my skull. He started to kiss at my mouth. The kiss was wet and disgusted me. He seemed rabid. He forced his tongue into my mouth as I tried to pull away. His actions assured me that I would be raped.

A knife quickly came into view. He held a black survival knife and a roll of twine. The weapons deactivated my fight-or-flight response, although they had not yet hurt me. Their presence was fear-inspiring.

So many thoughts raced through my mind and were then interrupted by new thoughts. My emotional symptoms were indicative of shock.

My hands were aggressively forced behind my back. Twine was wrapped tightly around my wrists. Once he tied my binds, he used more twine to further secure his bondage of me. His technique ensured I would not escape.

He drove with caution. My mind frantically searched for answers.

"Is this a joke?" I couldn't comprehend this hell to be reality. *How can this be real?* I thought. *This cannot be real.*

Shock and confusion are two emotions that do not work well together.

"Please talk to me. Is this a joke?" I looked at him with horror on my face.

"Shut up." He drove and seemed in control of the situation.

"Please." My legs kicked up and down on the floorboards as I squirmed in my seat.

"Shut up, whore." These words were blasted at me anytime I spoke enough to upset him. He kept one hand on the wheel and the other ready to strike.

The confusion worsened. If I could figure out why this was happening, I could understand it better. Thoughts and questions raced through my mind. *What did I do wrong? Why is he doing this to me? I am a good person! Children with disabilities depend on me for care. My life is dedicated to helping others. What did I do to deserve this?*

My eyes scoured him. "Is this about the phone number? I'm sorry. I'll go to breakfast with you."

"Shut up, whore."

Cars whizzed by us. It was bizarre to me that I was in this horrific situation, but no one knew. They just drove on with no knowledge of what was about to happen to me. The uncertainty of my circumstances made me quiver.

"Are you going to rape me?"

His lips were sealed.

"Are you going to rape me?" It sounded different the second time. My voice was weak at the end. When my desperate tactics failed, I changed my plan.

"You can rape me. Okay? But just don't hurt me." My words poured out quickly. "Yes, you can rape me, but don't hurt me, just let me go, I won't tell."

The man continued to drive.

"People on their way to work are going to see me and call the cops. I know a lot of people in this town."

He reached for a hat with sunglasses nested inside. He put the sunglasses on my face and the hat on my head.

Sarcasm was my new ploy. "A hat and sunglasses? They can still recognize me with a hat and sunglasses on."

"Shut up, bitch!" He reached over and double-checked the lock on the passenger door. He fastened my seat belt and laid my seat all the way back.

There were no more words. I just looked at the sky and began to accept my fate. The man drove toward the empty desert. He seemed to have a plan. While he drove, he reached over and unfastened my seatbelt. He unzipped his pants.

"Suck it."

The sight of his knife made me concede without hesitation. His penis did not seem to work; it just laid there. My hands were still secured tightly behind my back. My failed attempt to perform oral sex upset him. He pushed me away and punched me in the head numerous times and slammed his foot on the accelerator. Limp in my seat, I realized he drove faster to reach the destination because he was upset and couldn't wait to make me pay.

Under a minute later, he began to slow down. He scanned the deserted wasteland to his left. When he turned onto a gravel road, my heart sank into a place I had never known existed.

This field was well known. The road in was long, bumpy, and lined with telephone poles.

It was large and mostly abandoned, traveled only by men in white trucks who worked for the city and needed to fix telephone poles or by people with large junk to throw out, such as mattresses, refrigerators, and dishwashers. Not until I visited this enormous landfill did I ever imagine bodies could also be dumped there.

As the vehicle's tires met the dirt, I stared at the first telephone pole on the long road. Occasionally, I heard a rock bang the bottom of the car. Dust was the only thing that interrupted my view of the telephone poles to come. My brain scrambled all over the place, and I felt all of its cells ignite. My vision tunneled. Each telephone pole told me a story, and I listened intently. The first one told me that I would indeed be hurt. The second said that I would be raped. The third explained the horrifying experience was going to be worse than I imagined. Each pass of a telephone pole led us deeper into the isolated desert. The forth telephone pole told me I would never leave this desert, and the fifth said I'd be dumped like trash.

Unexplainably, I still felt *hope*—an ambition motivated by fear.

Once the poles in my view ended, the car came to a stop. The man put up my seat. We were far from civilization—the perfect place to commit a crime and not be caught.

He reached over and took off my shoes and struck me in the face with them. He pulled at my jean shorts; he grabbed his knife and cut at them. He eventually just used his hands to remove them because it would have taken too long to use the knife. He cut off my underwear. With his creepy little knife in hand, he reached under my oversized sweatshirt and cut off my bra.

It was then I knew he had done this before. He never attempted to remove my sweatshirt. Why would he? My hands were tied. It would not have come off. A novice would have tried. Every move the man made was calm, calculated, and precise.

He grabbed my underwear and forcibly shoved them into my mouth. His fingers were in my mouth and his other hand on the back of my head. As he pushed them into my throat, the pressure began to tear the corners of my mouth. I started to gag. He continued. My eyes began to water. By now, I had no thoughts; my body was just reacting to the pain. I cringed and twitched often. He tied the bra around my head to hold the underwear in place.

He moved his focus to his own body. He pulled his pants to his knees and climbed on top of me. He adjusted himself and attempted to rape me. With every part of my being, I bore down and tried not to feel the sexual activity. My mind went elsewhere. I stared out the window at a newspaper blowing in the wind as it desperately tried to escape its captor: a relentless bush.

The man became agitated and required my assistance. He could not perform. Rightfully, I was confused because I was not experienced in situations like this.

His eyes exuded an odious rage. The grim and deathlike black pits exposed a sinister past. No beauty dwelled within his soul, and that petrified me.

The devil demanded I tell him I love him. The first time I said these words with a sense of urgency, with absolutely no emotion behind them. I simply said, "I love you."

He punished me with a blow to the face. "Say it like you mean it."

I knew if it didn't sound right, all hell would break loose, so I took my time.

"Say it!" His words were like flames, scary and threatening.

"I love you." I trembled and looked away. These were words I had never said to anyone, not even my own parents. They were the hardest words in the world for me to say, and my life now depended on them.

He started to strangle me.

My body stiffened. My arms automatically raised mid-back. My instinct was to thrust him off, but my arms were still immobilized.

While his evil fingers squeezed the life from me, he again demanded that I say those words. Hoping he would let go, I moved my mouth to shape the letter "I" but paused. My jaw began to quiver, and my tongue began to thrust into my bottom teeth. I was dying.

"Gone"
Breath neither in nor out,
My thoughts squander as I pout.
God, is there a way to tell my friends and family to die, I'm about?
Inside my mind, I scream and shout.
Good-bye.
My eyes fill with white,
My heart pure delight,
My soul full of love.
I rise out, up, and above,
And I die.
No longer afraid,
No questions to ask,
My escape was contrite.
But now, I am back
Inside hell.

He brought me back to life. In a jolt, I was thrust back into my defeated body. With violence and force, he demanded my return. A rush of warmth filled my veins. Fear returned. After I realized I had just been murdered, I began to get antsy and move around.

As I sat in confusion, he started to lick and suck my neck. My body felt lifeless, and my mind was shot. His slobber ran down my neck and between my breasts. My soul was gone, and I could feel no pain. After a minute, he sat up and exposed his teeth full of blood. The man had tried to bite a chunk out of my neck.

He planned to kill me, and now I wanted to die. Death was seen as an escape, and the torture exhausted me. He opened the door and threw me onto the ground.

He opened his pants again and told me to perform oral sex. While on my knees, I considered biting his nasty penis off but was disgusted by the imagery. Instead, I fell back down and refused his command.

"No!" My heels pushed through the dirt and kicked up dust. He fought me to a standing position.

"Kill me!" I yelled.

The mood changed instantly when I no longer pleaded for my life. He simply left me and walked around the car. He popped open the trunk from inside his driver's door. As I watched from a point of shock, he reached into the trunk and pulled out a bag of knives. The doubled-up, brown shopping bag overflowed with blades protruding from the top. My heart dropped, but a split-second decision caused me to run.

Civilization was too far, but I did not run to find freedom. I ran, silently begging him to shoot me. The sight of the knives terrified me so much that I fled from my hellish desolate trap, with my arms tied behind my back, wearing nothing but a sweatshirt. My eyes squinted in anticipation of a swift bullet through the head.

As the wind beat my face, a powerful force struck the back of my head, and I fell. It took me a moment to realize that I was not dead. The man captured me and dragged me all the way back to the car, through the cactus and rocks, by my hair.

Back at the car, he pulled me to my feet. The gun was in his hand.

"Shoot me. Just kill me, you moron."

He grabbed my head and shoved the gun into my mouth. I squinted. The anticipation of death conquered my fears. He pushed the gun deeper inside my mouth. It made me blink and tense up more than I already was. He was toying with me. More than once, I imagined the back of my head blowing off. While I prepared for certain death, he decided to change the plan. He pulled the gun out of my mouth, pistol-whipped me, and began to fight me toward the trunk.

With no hands to assist me, I teetered on the back of the trunk. My legs would be my only tool to fight him. As I raised my legs to kick him, he pulled them up, and I fell into the trunk onto my back. I noticed a large angry raven on top of a telephone pole. As the trunk closed, the bird let out a loud, ferocious *squawk*. Then my world went black.

Me at age nineteen

Me at age nineteen

CHAPTER TWELVE

Lit

These were the days cars had no trunk releases.
Car manufacturers installed trunk release mechanisms in 1997,
seven years after my abduction. The slogan "Stranger Danger"
came out in the sixties, but I ignored it due to the irony
of my childhood existence.

The air reeked of pure evil. The horror of the moment snatched the soul from my body. My fate was now sealed in the trunk of the devil's car. On death's doorstep, I lay with my hands cinched behind my back. I couldn't even grope the pitch-black space around me, much less do anything other than entertain the paralyzing thoughts that rammed through my mind. Aroused by trepidation, I prepared for my imminent butcher.

Asphyxiation was a death I had already suffered. Now I would be decapitated, and rabid coyotes would devour my mangled body. As my friends and family rested cozy in their beds, I would be mutilated. These were the speculations I was forced to endure.

Motivated by fear, I thrashed inside my aluminum coffin. Panic set in, followed by hyperventilation. When I tried to cry, I couldn't. Instead, I let out crippled howls. Then, in a loud whisper, I began to interrogate myself.

"What do I do? *What* do I do?" My eyes zoomed all around the lightless trunk.

"What do I *know* about this?" I battled my impulse to panic, as a sense of urgency provoked the secretion of massive amounts of adrenaline.

I screamed. "What do I know?" With my teeth tightly clenched, I rolled my face into the trunk's bottom.

"Help, help, help, help, help," I whispered in a multitude of breathy voices.

With darkness all around me, I remembered something my grandma had told me when I was a child. She said, "Jenny, if you are ever in danger, pray. In Jesus's name, you should pray."

My eyes widened with this realization, and I grew spastic. My yelps developed a tone of hope. *How do I pray?* I wondered. *Just put your hands together, that's all.*

Suddenly, I felt as though I had a secret weapon. My fingers interlaced with fragile strength behind my back, and I summoned God. With every pause in my plea, I searched for his presence, my voice like an instrument not sure of its tune.

"God, I know you are there. Please, help me. I don't want to die. God? God, *if there is a God,* show yourself. Show yourself! Help me now or kill me. Kill me then … I don't want to be chopped up, God. Please help. If you exist, if you truly exist, help me. God! In Jesus's name …"

When tears would not flow, I tried to fake cry out of frustration, occasionally sounding like a wounded animal. My legs were restless, but I held them still. It was difficult to stifle my squirminess.

"God, please save me. I will tell everyone you saved me. Please, Lord. Please."

My energy was lost. Either I was depleted or I had lost all hope.

Suddenly, I felt adrenaline flood my body. My strength was hysterical. My confidence was at one hundred percent. To my astonishment, I heard the tension of the twine as it prepared to break. It popped three times, and my hands were set free.

The entire trunk ordeal lasted about fifteen minutes. At minute seven, I had regained the use of my hands and arms. Within another minute, I started to panic again. The twine no longer restricted the movement of my arms, but I was still sealed inside the trunk.

My momentary salvation was replaced with fright as I realized that I could not escape the trunk. Fantasies of what was to come began to control my uncertain emotions. My breathing was rapid and fast, and I faced the darkness in sheer distress.

At minute nine, logical visions of what would happen when the trunk opened horrified me so much that I decided to take my own life. With options exhausted and twine as my noose, I repented.

"God, if you exist, you know why I am doing this. Please forgive me."

My fingers gripped the ends of the twine, and I wrapped it around my neck. My hands pulled with what little energy remained in my body. Undamaged by my efforts, I spoke to God.

"Take me, Lord," I begged at minute ten as I strained my once-useless arms. All of my strength was used to no avail. No options were left; I would be murdered.

Finally, I succumbed to my circumstances. At minute eleven, I considered myself dead.

"Please, Lord, don't let me feel any of it," I whispered, while I held my hands folded in front of my eyes.

Suddenly, all was calm. Through the trunk, I saw a hand. A larger-than-life vision that instantly piqued my curiosity. It was not of this world. As I watched intently, the hand exposed a key. The key was placed into the lock on the outside of the trunk and was turned. The trunk was illuminated by either God or my imagination, and I saw how the lock operated. The mechanism that unlocked the trunk was on the inside with me. The latch of liberation was hidden between God's hand and the carpeted siding in the trunk. All the answers were given to me. After I reached my arms out to find the sides of the trunk, I met them in the center. My left hand was a marker, and my right hand tore the carpet at the corner. I peeled it from the metal, until my active hand could slide beneath. My fingers felt circular cutouts in the trunk's frame, and I pushed my hand into one near the middle.

I found the latch and turned it. Light flooded the trunk. Deliverance was at my fingertips. All my fear escaped out the cracks that led to my freedom.

The man drove fast. *If I raise the trunk, he will pull over,* I thought as I thrust the lid open. He noticed immediately but seemed confused.

"Wha— Wha— I'll shoot the backseat out!" He made an aggressive swerve off the road and came to a stop.

As I listened, I held the lid down to pretend it was shut. Suddenly, the trunk lid rose, and a gun was in my face. With my fingers pinching the lid, I pulled it hard. The slam of the trunk on his arm forced the man to retreat. During our brief struggle, the trunk was locked. My right hand stayed within the outer wall of the trunk, but I no longer felt the latch. The man bounced the car with his weight on the trunk, then tried to lift it to ensure the lid was closed completely.

In the darkness, I followed his sounds with my eyes. My destiny was about to change because I knew I would get out. I imagined the love I'd receive post-escape. My thoughts were fast.

Everyone will love me now. They will all cry and hug me. They will nurture and protect me. The media will interview me and commend my bravery and ask for my advice on how to escape from evil monsters. My life will change for the better, which will make this death-defying experience worth it. I will be a hero!

As I felt for the latch to reopen the trunk, I saw all of the beauty that awaited my arrival. My spirit was lit, pure, like the white light I previously witnessed. Determination and purpose now filled my veins. I was focused. The car was still. The back wheels began to spin. Purposely, I bounced the car so the back tires would dig deeper. As I bounced, I listened. The man pushed on the gas and muttered underneath his breath. He was panicked. He was stuck in the soft sand with a bloody, half-naked woman in his trunk and a bag of blades in the backseat.

He must have thought, *What if someone notices I'm stuck and pulls over to help me? What do I do then?*

When I put myself in his head now, I know he must have been terrified, and that thought makes me happy. Like any warrior does, I play the experience in my head, over and over, and fantasize different outcomes. Sometimes I imagine scenarios that make me cringe, while others make me laugh until I nearly pee myself. As a survivor, these cognitive illusions are essential to preserve your sanity. They also bear a gift—power.

Stuck in the sand, he quickly developed a routine. After he pushed the gas pedal, he would turn his head and yell at me. His words did not matter; I was focused on his patterns. He yelled at me, turned and focused on the traffic, then attempted to accelerate. To my advantage, his wheels continued to rotate hopelessly in the sand.

After timing his actions, I waited for him to yell toward the trunk. My hand had found the trunk's release again. As his attention averted back to the traffic, I threw the trunk open and jumped out. Immediately I knew I was in trouble; my hand was stuck within the wall of the trunk. I considered leaving it behind. The opening of his door motivated me enough to dislodge my hand. At minute fifteen, I was free.

Ravaged, I fled toward oncoming traffic that did not exist. Cars in the distance were too tiny to make out. In my entire life, I had never run this fast. I was one with the wind and far from myself. My legs were no longer felt beneath me. Occasional zigzags were thrown into my flight to ward off any potential bullets.

Then, to my right, a vehicle began to cruise alongside me. The driver's side mirror was the nearest thing to grab, as the car never decreased its speed. An elderly couple, reminiscent of my grandparents, suddenly appeared as my saviors. As I peeled my hands off the mirror and grasped for the opened window, the woman in the passenger seat became hysterical.

As she looked toward the backseat and out the back window, she open-handedly struck her husband. There was a look of horror on her already-pale face.

"Go! Go!" she yelled.

The driver sped up as I frantically lunged toward the window. My grip was lost, but my hope was still intact. There was no time for negativity now. Yet the thought of what the woman witnessed discouraged me greatly. The more I told myself not to look back, the more curious I became. With no knowledge of the distance between us, I turned to find the man chasing me down the middle of the road with a machete.

Chapter Thirteen

That's What You Get for Hitchhiking

"Free"
Desert birds sang.
Medical professionals, firefighters, and cops cried.
Sure, it was unprofessional, but they couldn't help it.
They were only human.
My mom ran to me in a teary-eyed panic.
She apologized for every awful thing she'd ever done to me.
She was kind and nurturing.
She wanted to protect me.
My horror was worth her love.
Finally, I was free of danger.

As I ran, I raised my arms out and chest up like a diver posing atop a board. My head tilted upward a bit. My eyes were invisibly tethered to a delusion so brilliant, only I could see it.

As I rose off the ground, I began to fly, my feet gently brushing along the asphalt. This was the moment I longed for. The world as I knew it was about to change forever because I would either die or ignite. My fuel, the love and admiration of others. The spark, aspirations I held within. The world was good. The man was bad. These were the feelings I had as I ran.

A large object began to approach me. My eyes pierced right through it. A dream world had formed to protect me. A truck appeared and startled my daze. The fear of rejection struck me like a dagger, but I ran toward the truck with my eyes closed. I heard a screech. The truck had stopped for me. A rush of adrenaline persuaded me to attack the driver's window like a destructive wild animal. The passenger jumped out of the truck and rushed toward me.

"We are marines," he said as he reached out to help and took in my appearance.

Like a wild animal, I could not talk; I was only capable of horrendous noises. Concern overtook him, and he huddled me into the backseat of the truck.

The mistake of trusting a stranger had nearly cost me my life; now, it was saving my life. My disabled mind found no irony in that. No mental or physical strength was left for an outcome that would require it. My fight was gone. I merely existed at this point.

My eyes zoomed in and through the most random objects, unaware of what they viewed, and led me to a place of confusion. My soul attempted to escape its physical imprisonment through my vision.

My control center was only responsive when questioned loudly or repeatedly. Touch felt like electricity; it would startle me, even when I saw it coming.

When I was silent, I was elsewhere, and when I spoke, I was everywhere. Words spewed from my mouth, like water from a defective fountain. My voice radiated through my hollow mind. I felt its vibration but could not make out the words it tried to convey. My face preformed a multitude of expressions, exerting muscles I didn't know existed.

Humiliation makes you humble. I had forgotten that I was nearly naked. An oversized sweatshirt hung on my body, but there was no other clothing.

"He was going to murder me!" I shouted as I put on a new pair of Levi pants the guys handed me.

"Who?"

I pointed my finger. "Him!" The man was now unstuck, barreling down the road far ahead of us.

"Get him!" I shouted. "He had me in the trunk! Get him!"

"What truck?" the passenger asked in a panic.

"The trunk! In the trunk! He kidnapped me!" I screamed.

"What?" the driver shouted as he slammed the accelerator to the floor.

He drove fast in an attempt to catch the car. The marines' anger toward the killer made me feel loved. They wanted to make him pay. Now I was along for the ride.

The driver's eyes were focused on the road ahead, and the passenger was bent forward as if he couldn't catch the man fast enough. He tapped the front window aggressively.

"That car, there?" He rubbed his fists as if to condition them for a fight.

"Yes!" I throttled his headrest. "Get him! He bit me!"

The kidnapper sped through the stop sign.

"He strangled me!" I yelled.

We were about two blocks behind him.

"What's his build?"

"He's small."

"Does he have any weapons?"

"Yes! A gun, a knife! Bag—a bag of knives!" I sounded like a frantic contestant on a game show. "Blades! Blades everywhere." My hands moved in the air as if I were playing charades. "Blades were sticking out!"

The men looked at each other repeatedly. They did not speak.

My hands measured the invisible bag. "A big bag! And a gun! Did I say gun?"

The truck suddenly lost its momentum. My eyes witnessed a silent communication between the two men.

Confused, I yelled with all the strength I could muster. "Go!"

"A gun and knives?" the driver asked. He took one hand off the wheel and adjusted his body toward me.

"What? Go!" My forehead scrunched into a frozen state. "Yes, but he is small."

The car in the distance turned onto a side road.

"He turned! Go faster!" I screamed as I slapped the passenger's leather seat.

He abruptly turned toward me. "We can't. This is a job for the police," he said.

"No!" I pressed my face into the window beside me. "He went that way." I pointed as we passed his turn.

"We will stop at a gas station and call the police," the driver said.

In disbelief, I spun in my seat and stared out the back window with eyes full of tears, until I could no longer see.

About twelve minutes later, we entered a town I knew well— Morongo Valley, the town I grew up in. We pulled into the gas station, and I saw people I recognized in the parking lot. The drop of my heart reminded me I had one. People in town knew the story of my childhood, that I grew up with no water or electricity. Now they were about to find out that someone tried to murder me.

We parked near the double glass doors of the entrance. The marines sheltered me into the store. As I walked in, I stared at my dirty bare feet and wondered who noticed me. The driver alerted the attendant of the emergency, and I was guided by him into a small office to use the telephone. As I spoke to the 911 operator, the marines disappeared, never to be seen again.

Moments later, paramedics appeared. Everyone around me spoke loudly. A gurney was pulled inside the office, and I was secured onto it. Medical professionals began to rapid-fire their questions.

"What's your name, hun?"

"Jen … ni … fer," I said, as if it hurt to talk. I covered my face with my hands.

"What's that?" My hands were removed from my face. "Can you

speak up, hun?"

"Jen … nifer," I answered again. Embarrassed, I turned away from the lookie-loos that now gathered around the ambulance.

Before they asked me for my last name, I heard a voice that was comfortingly familiar.

"Well. She is quite the storyteller," the voice said.

My mom leaned against a police car and casually sipped a Pepsi. Frantic, I cried out for her. She strolled toward me with a look of disgust on her face, as if I had done something horribly wrong. When she was close enough to reach, I tried to cling on to her arm.

"I was kidnapped, Mom!" I yelled, causing the crowd to gasp and murmur.

My mom had all eyes on her. "Well, that's what you get for hitch-hiking," she replied as she released herself from my grips. She walked away, and my gurney was lifted into the ambulance. The air held my hand for comfort as my heart shattered.

Of course, the ambulance ride was a blur. You see, when my mom spoke those words, my eyes altered. While open, they broke into a billion little pieces, and in these pieces, I could see the universe mixed with any beautiful memory I ever had. Then there was a shift.

Distant experiences erupted from my soul and uncontrollably purged through my vision: the stoic policemen's faces, the paramedic intently focused on spelling my name right, my mother.

The child in me had been murdered. She no longer existed. No one cared about me like they had when I was a child. At the time I needed it most, everyone in the world turned on me. These people only cared about my physical injuries—the bloody bite mark on my neck and my torn-up wrists. No one asked or cared how I was. I felt lost inside my own body.

The visions I had, when I ran for my life, were wrong. Not one person acted how they were supposed to act. No one hugged me, no one nurtured me, nobody cared. They all wore masks and performed only tasks required by law. Robots. The world was evil.

The world was evil, and I was the pitiful "scapegoat" for all of the monsters on earth to victimize.

MY LIGHT WAS GONE. I questioned if the light I thought I had was ever even real. I wondered if the light I saw in other people's eyes was, in fact, ignited by me or was just an illusion. All eyes were now black because my soul had gone blind.

The salaried angels spoke in code as they transcribed the severity of my physical trauma. My pulse and blood pressure readings were unexceptional, and my wounds were superficial.

My heart and soul were never examined, though they suffered the most trauma. My heart was ruptured and bleeding heavily. My soul was lost inside my body, its only desire was to engage or escape. Without emotional connection, it shuddered aimlessly through my body, searching for an outlet in which to depart.

At the hospital, my story was told for me as I listened. The many versions perked my interest and desensitized my mind. The accounts varied from "she claims some man hurt her" to "apparently she believes he wanted to kill her." No one knew what I had experienced, and unfortunately, no one cared.

Occasionally, I began to float adrift in my mind, only to be physically jolted back to reality. From the hospital bed, my attention could only be alerted with physical touch or the announcement of my name—not Jennifer, but "Ms. Asbenson." In the span of a few hours, I heard my last name more times than I had ever heard it in high school PE classes. It was a name I did not respond to. Reactions came quick when I heard it, but only because I thought it was in reference to my mom. "Ms. Asbenson" was her name, not mine, and as soon as it exited a mouth, I would frantically look around the room for her. Eventually,

I realized she was not coming. I would face this trauma alone.

After my veins sucked up the IV fluid that I probably did not need and I received a rape kit test, I found myself in a small treatment room with five police officers. No treatments were offered. Agitated and now fearful of men, I did not make eye contact. I looked at the ground while I sat in a school-style plastic chair and witnessed the commotion.

"How do you know he was going to kill you?" a badged-suited man asked.

A *badged-suited man* is a typical man, until he dresses for work and leaves his home. He is a man who has left all of his emotions at home, a man in search of "details" and "statements." In this case, he was a detective—a frustrated official in search of facts.

"Did he tell you he was going to kill you? Did he say that, Ms. Asbenson?"

I looked up. "Yes. He said he was going to murder me and chop me into a million pieces."

The room fell silent.

I slowly uttered my next words: "That's what he said." I looked down toward the floor.

In disbelief, the men jotted notes.

Now, you and I both know that the deranged man never said those words. In an effort to convince the badged-suited men of the severity of the crime, I lied. When they questioned me, they did not take me seriously. In order to assure the madman's capture and in an attempt to save future victims' lives, I misled them.

As they cross-examined me, I had to occasionally remind myself that my hands were not still secured behind my back. The men paced the room and looked at me with inquisitive eyes.

"Do you find this funny, Ms. Asbenson?" one of them asked.

He pointed to his briefcase. "I've got photos in there of a woman who was chopped into pieces and shoved into buckets." He gritted his teeth. "A real victim."

When he said *chopped*, he sawed at the air, as if I needed help picturing the massacre. The images in my head disturbed me little, as the world had already transformed into hell.

After a while, I grew tired of the questions, but they continued. The "nice cop" took his turn.

"Ms. Asbenson, if this was your boyfriend, just tell us. Perhaps the two of you got into a disagreement?" he asked.

The last question forced my eyes to focus on the ground more so that my mind could escape to somewhere better. Sixty minutes prior to being mind-fucked, I sat in a white treatment chair and gazed at the ceiling. The room smelled of rubbing alcohol. My bottom half was naked, and a blue paper dress, with the back open, rested on my top parts. My legs were spread wide open. I was gone from my thoughts. A long cotton swab scrapped the insides of my vagina. Humiliation was not felt; no emotions were present. My body had caused me so much pain that I began to despise it.

The soft voice of a woman told me that all would be okay. A hand softly touched my hand, and I pulled away. The voice told me that she understood and that what happened to me was horrible. She was the only compassionate person I had encountered so far. She must have learned my story from the others, because I never told her. I had no idea what version she received, and I never asked.

My glossed-over eyes recognized compassion in hers. Somehow, she was able to leave her mask at home. She was *real*, and she truly cared. Her kindness was not enough to help my heart, and my soul was too far gone, but I did take notice. I asked for her name.

"My name is Alice," she calmly replied.

Alice? I thought. *That's kind of strange.* I had never met another Alice before. My body felt dead as she performed the rape kit test on me. The name Alice repeated over and over in my head until the test concluded.

ONE OF THE BADGED-SUITED MEN stepped toward me as I pondered the name Alice.

"Well, Ms. Asbenson, this is my card."

It's so ironic that that was her name, I thought.

"Ms. Asbenson?"

Maybe she loved me.

"If you think of anything else, give us a call."

I ARRIVED HOME AT SUNDOWN. Exhausted, I stumbled into my apartment. Tyler was there with another one of my girlfriends. They had already heard the story, but I told them my version too. Because of how I had been treated, I figured my own friends wouldn't believe me either. It was difficult for me to be in the apartment. The maniac initially picked me up at a liquor store about a block from my apartment, so he could probably find me with little effort, especially since I didn't have a car.

That night, I could not sleep. On top of NyQuil, I drank two beers. Because I was too afraid to lie down, I leaned against the wall and watched my friends sleep. The television kept me company. The thought that no one did enough to help me drove me crazy. My heart began to race as I imagined the crazy man about to bang down the front door and murder me once and for all.

In a panic, I grabbed the landline telephone, dragged it into the bathroom, and locked myself in. The bathroom was tiny; it had one toilet, a sink, and a shower. I felt safe wrapped in a blanket in the shower, with the plastic curtain on one side and a wall with a small window, too small for the man to fit through, on the other.

The phone sat on my lap as I thought about the new Alice. She had given me her card, but I had not yet looked at it. *Rape Crisis Center*, it read. My hand trembled as I tried to recall if I was actually raped. *If I was not raped, could I still call?* I wondered. I tried to think deeper. *I don't remember the feeling of something going inside me. I did push, though. I pushed out with my body and my breath because that was the only thing I could do to reject what was happening to me. It was like I was trying to blow him away with my body. I protected my mind at that point, so well that I don't know if I was raped or not.*

Earlier in the day, a police officer had asked me if I was penetrated. I asked him what that meant; I didn't know. Sex lingo was not a subject area I excelled in; I was not experienced. All I knew was that the killer became upset in his attempts, and his penis seemed to have a problem with firmness. It didn't matter to me if I had been raped or not. I would have felt robbed either way.

After rewinding my mind and examining my memory about the rape, I decided to call. It was two o'clock in the morning. A young girl answered. She sounded like I woke her up.

"Rape Crisis Center."

At that point, no words would leave my mouth. She sighed as if no one who called her ever spoke right away. She waited for a response.

I flipped the light switch off so that the kidnapper wouldn't be able to see me through the small shower window. I didn't want anyone to hear me either.

"I was raped. I was kidnapped and raped," I said.

"Okay, so you were raped?" She was not very professional. It sounded like she was preoccupied with something in the background, so I freaked out on her.

My hand shook. "Help me, please! He is a murderer! He is going to kill other girls!"

"Okay, if you want me to help you, you need to calm down."

"Where is Alice?" I asked.

"Alice is not here."

Confused, I started to cry. I pulled the phone closer to my ear when I heard a new noise. It was a dial tone. She had hung up on me.

THE BATHROOM BECAME MY SAFEHOUSE for the next few days. I'd only leave when someone needed to use it. Sometimes, though, I would stay; it really depended on what they wanted to use the bathroom for.

One night, I decided to try and act normal, so I watched TV with my roommate. Not long after a show started, I walked into the kitchen to get some water. As I lifted the glass to my mouth, it slipped and shattered all over the floor. The next thing I knew, I was on the ground. I lay on my back on top of the glass pieces and convulsed, like I was having a grand mal seizure. Slobber began to slip from my mouth as my eyes rolled into my head.

Worried and with no idea what to do, my friend called 911. The paramedics arrived quickly and loaded me up for the hospital. I was unresponsive, but I could see and hear all that occurred.

The hospital staff recognized me as the same girl who had come in a few days prior. The entire time, I shook with no control and hoped it meant I would die. Unable to communicate, I listened to the frantic banter of the nurses.

"She claimed she was kidnapped."

"Is she having a seizure?"

"No!"

"Maybe she just likes attention."

"They never found the guy."

"Mental breakdown?"

"Ma'am! Stay still!"

"Don't poke yourself, Sheila!"

"We need restraints over here!"

"That should do it!"

"You get her?"

"Looks like it."

Then complete and utter silence.

The next day, I awoke to find myself strapped to a bed in a mental institution.

Police photo, after I was kidnapped.
The cuts on my wrists were all that reminded me of the truth.

CHAPTER FOURTEEN

5150

The treehouse has a new addition. The structure sits a foot below the entrance of my eight-by-eight-square-foot treehouse. A few weeks ago, I constructed a ten-by-ten deck by myself. It looked like a large wooden wall when I finished. The man in the house helped me put nine four-foot posts under the deck for support. Cement blocks secure the legs in place. At first, the completed project looked like a stage, but it served no purpose, so I covered the deck to create a room.

The E-Z UP on top creates a roof. The skinny-legged canopy was drilled down so that it couldn't take off in the wind. There were no walls, so I created those out of bamboo—bamboo fencing to be specific. When the day is hot, I water the tall hollow sticks with a hose, and when the wind blows, the air is cooled.

In the middle of the deck is a queen-size airbed. Above the bed is a solar-paneled, black chandelier. Mental disorders on folded sticky notes dangle from the yarn I hung from it. The new invention resembles a mobile over a baby's crib. The pastel-colored papers blow in the wind like tiny upside-down kites. They begin to tangle with one another, creating a bunch of "mental problems." It's mesmerizing. Sometimes I feel like I could gaze at it forever …

As I lie on the magical bed in my humble treehouse, I travel back—back to when I thought my life was over, back to when I was companionless and confused. During that time in my life, when I closed my eyes, I was forced to visualize myself somewhere else, a place like where I am now—warm, even when cold. I would picture myself at a beautiful destination with hymns and Christmas lights or any other place I felt safe, where everyone believed me and loved me.

And if they didn't, it wouldn't matter, because I believed and loved myself.

You can only gaze at a ceiling for so long before you begin to feel crazy. Some would say I was already nuts, since the ceiling I stared at occupied the skies of a mental institution. There are few possibilities for entertainment in such a place. As long as you have a mind, you have choices. I chose to count the dots and pretend the rain spots were dark clouds; that seemed to keep my mind off the situation.

When you cannot hear noise, you tend to use your other senses more. Touch was constrained, so I chose vision. My feet faced the west toward the door. Tears rolled down my cheeks and into my ears. It was an all-time low.

My skin looked blue. Maybe I was dead. Most likely I was just cold since I had no blankets. My palms faced the floor. My hands laid outstretched, like little stars, and gently trembled as the eyes in my tilted head admired them. I was strapped to a bed. But the small white room—my room—felt secure.

My new negative imagination told me I would die here ... not in this room, but in this psychiatric ward with all its creeps and weirdos. These snake pits were evil places. Patients were shocked with electric volts, tortured, and given lobotomies. Every moment, I yearned for someone to bust through the door and save me, but unfortunately, that someone did not exist.

Why didn't the psychiatric hospital feel more like my treehouse? Warm and comfortable. Secure and sure. Why was it painted the same color everywhere? Stark white, with no decoration. Cold and lonely. No art. Not an ounce of visual stimuli. Nothing emotionally enticing. No intrigue. Just a lonely and perverted, highly-secured structure meant to confine the misunderstood and unloved rejects of the world.

The worst part of all of this was accepting that I was, in fact, one of them.

My new psychologist told me I was being held on a "5150." It was a three-day hold. A doctor from the hospital recommended I be confined for seventy-two hours because I was a danger to myself.

Apparently, I was suicidal. The slashes on my wrists and my erratic behavior told a "medically obvious" sad story. My freshly medicated mind assured me his words were the truth. My cuts were not from the imaginary twine; they were indeed self-inflicted, he said. Out of the blue, I had lost my mind and made up a story that someone tried to kill me. I then slit my wrists and hoped to die. My mind was boggled as I tried to debate the wild accusations, and then my voice disappeared.

A few days prior, my voice began to trip up when I spoke. I assumed it was laryngitis, but my mind occasionally played tricks on me. I'd see sadistic images of a madman with his fingers tight around my neck, causing vocal cord damage.

Schizophrenia can come on quickly, I was told. The psychologist assured me that I could no longer tell the difference between fantasy and reality. Medications existed that could fix this. More days within these confined walls would help, they said. So I was sentenced to a longer stay.

How had this happened to me? Why would I suddenly have delusions of such an awful thing? Maybe I made it all up for attention because I felt unloved. I *was* a storyteller. I'd been in a fantasy world all of my life, but I knew the difference between real and pretend, didn't I? It didn't matter anyway because I was not prepared to tell the scary story anymore. The horrific events were not only painful to tell, but once told, the details only caused more agony.

In the community room of the loony bin, cradled by a worn plastic chair, I studied the nut-jobs. I sat with my feet on the seat and my knees bent near my chin in a protective position. My arms were wrapped around my legs to shield my vulnerable heart.

As the weirdos lined up for medication, I gaped. If I waited until the line cleared, I'd feel ordinary. To stand in a line at your own will and accept a cure-all that only made you crazier seemed insane.

My first dinner in the asylum was bizarre. As one guy ate, he threw the contents of his meal tray. His food landed on an unhinged woman's plate, and she screamed loudly and refused to eat. Another guy stood up, stepped away from the table, spread his legs, and peed himself as he laughed. His urine splashed on the ground, and he kicked at it. Some patients watched and continued to eat. One woman gawked and sang an awful song. During the entire meal, I tried not to gag.

Shower time was after dinner. If I wanted to shave my armpits or legs, I was observed. A nurse stood a few feet away and made sure I didn't kill myself with the plastic safety razor. Even if I wanted to kill myself, I'd find it difficult. Because of the high dose of medication, I could hardly stand. To avoid humiliation, I yet again escaped away in my mind. My shower escapes had been mastered by now.

The first two weeks went by fast. This kind of life was surreal because I had no voice. I was medicated so much that I never knew what day it was. All I lived for was food, showers, sleep, and medication.

While I slept, someone checked on me every hour. Sometimes when they checked on me, they would take the shoe off my back. This angered me because I had it there to pretend someone loved me. I imagined a kind friend or a loving family member had tucked me in, cuddled next to me, and put their hand on my back.

I always knew when a nurse came into my room because I slept lightly. When they entered, I pretended to be asleep. They would remove the shoe, and I would have to wait for them to leave. Then

I had to start my nightly routine all over again. Although I was frustrated when they removed the shoe, I began to expect the intrusion.

BECAUSE I SLEPT UPSIDE DOWN, the orderlies probably thought I had lost my marbles. It made sense to me, though. I did not sleep upside down like a bat; that would be bizarre. I slept on my stomach with my head on the opposite end of the bed.

In the outside world, I no longer slept in beds. But in the mental hospitals, I was told that if I didn't sleep in the bed, they would strap me to it. So I decided to sleep upside down instead. That way, if someone crept into my room and tried to murder me, they would stab at my legs instead of my heart. Brilliant safety ideas always came natural to me.

I MADE FRIENDS WITH A woman in the institution. Her name was Kristy. She was sweet, like me. She had bruises, scratches, and crusty blood on her body because she had leapt out of a moving car. Intrigued by her guts and courage, I instantly bonded with her. *Only a truly ballsy person would do that,* I thought. I couldn't understand why she made that choice because she seemed so reasonable.

Soon I realized she wasn't that normal. Every time I used the restroom after her, it would be decorated in toilet paper. Sometimes I became upset because she used it all. Her hands had touched the decorative toilet paper, so I refused to wipe my butt with it. I'd pop my head out the cracked door with my pants around my ankles and cry out until someone brought me a new roll. Kristy always denied it was her and acted completely sane, but I knew she was the guilty one. In a strange way, it made me like her more, even if she was an oddball.

It blows my mind as I sit here—with my candles glowing and my favorite song on repeat—and think about how long I spent in the hospitals. My life would have been a lot easier if the doctors had just offered me marijuana instead of medication. The medication made me lose track of time, and the years began to blend together.

For about four years, I lived in and out of mental institutions. I was a regular. Every time I visited, I'd be diagnosed with a new disorder. Once, the psychologists said I had obsessive-compulsive disorder. Simple things would drive me nuts. My unruly mind made me touch door handles over and over; I also frequently rechecked the sink nozzles to assure there were no drips.

One time, I called my mom repeatedly, like I was about to win a prize from the radio station. When she answered, I thought it was a new day, so I repeated the information I had told her during the previous phone call. At first, she laughed, but then she said I was psychotic and delusional, and if I wasn't, I wouldn't be at the funny farm. So I hung up, added her new diagnoses to my list of ailments, and never called her again.

My friends and family did not visit me. It was probably hard enough for them to watch me go crazy. On visitation days, I pretended to get excited like everyone else.

Once, I heard that many writers are also drinkers. This makes sense to me because the emotional pain of revisiting the past is sometimes unbearable. The lipstick stain on my wine glass reminds me of the time I lied to the girls at the desk behind the thick glass window and told them I had a visitor so that they would use their makeup on me. Red lipstick made me look irresistible, and I paraded around for hours before visitation ended.

One time, Mr. Pee-Pee Pants's family came to visit him, and they brought a baby along. As I sat with my combed wet hair and blinding red lipstick, I stared at the baby. I wondered why I wasn't born into a loving family. Envious of the large-eyed and blond-haired girl, I examined her every move. When the family stood up to leave at the end of the night, I saw the baby's bottle on its side behind a chair. My mouth began to open to alert them, but I quickly decided against the idea. It was my prize. When they left, I hid the bottle under my sweatshirt and brought the little treasure to my room. After I filled it up with water, I nursed myself to sleep. This made me feel warmth and love, just as a baby would. When I awoke in the morning, the baby bottle was gone and the shoe had been removed from my back. *If I never noticed them enter, I must have slept well,* I thought.

MEDICATIONS MADE ME FEEL LIKE a carefree zombie. As I dragged my squeaky tennis shoes over the shiny white floor, my fingers skimmed along the endless walls. Sometimes I'd do this so much my fingertips would become sore. If I complained about the pain, I would receive pain pills. Once one of the freaks got mad at me because my shoes were too noisy. From then on, my daily wall obsession was a barefoot expedition.

AFTER THE COLLAPSE AT MY apartment, and in between mental hospital visits, I moved back in with my parents. At night, I only felt safe if I slept on the roof, like I did with Tyler as a kid, or under my bed. My family thought I was crazy, but in case my story was indeed real, I didn't want the madman to find me and kill me as I slept.

About two months after being in and out of the hospitals, I returned to work. My dad gave me a pearlescent white Mazda RX-7. The car was beautiful. He did the body work on it himself. He had always planned to give all of us kids a car. Mine was a bit late but respectfully appreciated.

My boss suggested I work during the day for some reason, perhaps due to my newfound fear of the dark. On my first day back, I was confronted by a new employee who questioned me.

"So, you've worked here awhile?" she asked.

"Yes, about two years. I just took my vacation."

"Oh my gosh! So, did you hear about the girl who was kidnapped?"

My unblinking eyes stuck to the first distraction I could find. "A girl was kidnapped?"

"Yes, and raped."

My head moved as if weighted by an external force and began to sink into nonexistent soft sand. I spoke with heavy hesitation, "I think that was me."

She laughed. "You think?" She saw my unstable expression. "Wait. What? For real? That was you?"

No communication was left in me, so I walked away.

The girls were delighted to see me, but I wasn't as thrilled in return. I pondered why God would make them the way they were. As I looked at the precious girls' faces, I wondered why any of them were born.

While I bathed baby Violet, I pierced her eyes with mine. Her remarkable soul fled through her blinded eyes, but I could see she was trapped. As her tiny feet splashed the water, my mind began to drift. Unspeakable thoughts intruded my mind, but I was aware of the difference between right and wrong. *What would happen if I just let her go? Would she sink? Would she float? She was blind, deaf, and disabled. She couldn't do anything. Why was she alive? What was the purpose?*

My thoughts began to upset me. *Why did I process the world so differently?* Before the time of my sanity issues, I had focused on how I could make Violet's reality livable. Now I questioned why she even existed. As I ran clear water over her precious baby hair, my heart broke.

To avoid interaction with the girls, I demanded my night shift back. *The late shift shouldn't scare me if what I said happened was indeed made up*, I thought. The idea of the man coming back to finish the job—to finally kill me—sometimes crossed my mind, but I'd quickly remind myself that I might be nuts. With my new medications, I could try to get my life back on track. Never had I prayed so desperately to return to myself.

"Distant Soul"
When the self seems gone,
The soul cannot sing,
The heart cannot love.
Misery is king.
From the darkness you cry,
From the eyes that can't see,
From the depths of the doom,
You shall rise from defeat.
Cling on to the hope of the light you will see.
And that hope, one day,
Will indeed set you free.

Gone was the "ghost girl" who had romped after the girls in fresh, warm, white sheets. Absent were the joyrides and sweet treats of whipped cream. Deceased was the fire that fueled my desire to gleam.

Somber, I sat and stared at a large plain wall in the now woeful house. Memories of who I had been and the smiles I once created began to flood my mind. The costumes and masks, the bubbles and tricks were absent. No more were the times when the girls would dance as they helped me mop and vacuum. I no longer strove for the excellence frequently displayed before my vacation—like the time there was an earthquake. I was deemed a hero because I quickly arranged all of the girls on a bed and rolled them to the driveway to safety. Or the time Violet signed "eat" because I wouldn't give up on teaching her sign language, even though she was blind, deaf, and mentally fractured. Gone were those days.

The sheets were now folded and put away. The wheelchair was kept in the garage. Safety replaced fun. If you observed from the outside in, I would have looked like a very responsible employee.

Security lights and alarms were installed. The doors were locked at night. The house never felt safe enough. My frenzied mind made me double- and even triple-check them.

One night, as I mopped I heard a strange noise. With the mop as my weapon, I crept around the corner to find Christina with a huge smile on her face and her hand on the knob of the back door. My heart sunk.

"No! Christina! Christina, no. Do not open the door."

As I walked toward her, I spoke slowly. She began to wildly laugh and prance in place. She never spoke because she didn't know how. My voice changed to a mild tone.

"Christina. Come on, honey. Away from the door. Let's go back to night-night," I said.

She looked confused and took her hand off the knob. "Good girl, honey."

My eyes widened. "No!"

She flipped the lock and opened the door. She took off into the backyard.

Alarms wailed throughout the house. "No!" I yelled.

The thought of the dark yard attempted to cripple me, but I would let no harm come to these girls. I ran after her with the mop in hand. In rebellion, she laughed and danced while she covered her ears. Finally, I wrangled her in.

The phone began to ring. My thoughts ran rampant.

The two girls who could hear and walk flew out of their rooms in hysterics. One whimpered, and the other pet me roughly with her soaked fingers. The symphony of noise terrified them, as it did me.

The phone stopped ringing. After I pressed random numbers into the alarm box, I forced myself to breathe and remember the correct code. The alarm fell silent.

The phone began to ring again, and I informed the attendant on the other end that it was false. After I hung up, I dropped to the floor with the girls and cried. The doors were never opened again.

I sometimes imagined a lunatic was on the loose and he knew where I worked. No one at the house ever questioned me about the incident again, which I appreciated, since I wasn't even sure it had happened.

While experimenting with different medications, I began to feel like my life could go back to normal. At the same time, the drugs made me feel numb. I was in and out of various forms of reality. No matter how much I tried to escape the scary story, it would always try and prove itself to be real.

One morning before work, I enjoyed a hot shower. As I shampooed my hair, a message began to appear on the large bathroom window. The more the steam bellowed through the room, the brighter the message appeared. The words had been written with a finger.

Once I was able to read it clearly, I began to shake. With soap all over me, I grabbed a towel and ran out of the bathroom, screeching.

My mom looked at the window to see if what I told her was true. She saw the words as clear as day. A large handprint was beneath the three dreadful words "I WAS HERE."

He had been inside my home. I was not safe. No one was safe.

*Mental hospital gowns were so comfortable
that I often wore them at home*

CHAPTER FIFTEEN

The Beauty of Blood

Blood is beautiful when you examine it closely. A sense of calm falls upon you as you wait for it to appear; it's strange.

Before I would slit my wrists, I'd wash them. Sweet melancholy music played to ease my mind as I held the razor close to my eyes and examined it. The proof on my wrists was easily found. The seven bracelet-shaped scars, left from the twine, were the only evidence that kept my story alive.

The first time I cut, I was nervous. But soon, I fell in love. Never had I focused so intently or felt such a sense of control.

Like an artist with a thin brush, I gently swept the razor over my nearly healed scars. With my lips slightly separated and my pupils dilated, I peered closely as the blood began to seep to the surface. Somehow, the arrival of the blood caused the emptiness inside my body to vanish.

My eyebrows rose with childlike curiosity. The particular redness of the blood was so clean and beautiful. The crimson plasma stimulated my dreary mind. After I created one gash, I grew excited to inflict the next.

Nervous delight filled my stomach as I continued the spiritually satisfying ritual. The emotion I developed was comparable to waiting for a blind date to arrive. An excitable edginess elicited exactly what my mind needed.

WHEN THE POLICE WERE UNABLE to lift prints from the fogged-up window, I retreated to cutting. Of course, I sometimes imagined prodding deep enough to end my life. With my new mental ailments and my mind set, it took more *courage* to carry on in the world than it would have to off myself.

My post-traumatic stress disorder (PTSD) told me that when he finally caught me, I would be stabbed to death. The torturous visions flooded my mind all day. The act of cutting desensitized me to the sight of blood. It was no longer gore—the red fluid was beauty. If I saw it enough, I wouldn't panic when I was stabbed.

Normally, I'd only cut the seven scars that needed attention, but this time, I went overboard. The infliction of physical pain relieved my internal pain significantly.

On the left arm, I began to cut from my wrist to where my arm bent. On the right, I'd only cut the wrist. It was hard to cut the right arm because I am right-handed, and my left hand trembled when I tried to perform precise tasks with it.

To cover my fresh wounds, I cut the feet out of socks and pulled the tubes over my hands and up my arms to my elbows, like arm warmers. As I walked near my mom in the house, I hid my special secret. Similar to caring for a hurt, helpless creature, the comfort derived from nurturing the wounds was intoxicating.

When you commit an act of harm to yourself without anger in your heart, it is a strangely beautiful experience, perhaps like the drip of hot wax onto the flesh. There is a thrill, a high associated with it. When you feel like you have lost control of everything else, any control is welcomed, and I had control when I cut.

One evening, a cut-induced high was interrupted by a friend who barged into the bathroom. I ended up back in the looney bin on another 5150. Apparently I was suicidal, although my cutting was not intended to be lethal. Quite simply, it was the only thing in the world that had the ability to make me feel again. When I was seemingly numb to emotional pain, I discovered physical pain.

The razor became my best friend because I was lonely. Being misunderstood made me feel so isolated and withdrawn that when I cut, I felt alive.

Me at nineteen, trying to look like a movie star

CHAPTER SIXTEEN

The Fascinating Freaks

After about six months in and out of mental hospitals, the institutions began to feel like home. The familiar faces gave me a sense of security. Somehow, I gained the ability to tell myself that I was okay in there. When I closed my eyes, I could imagine I was in a fancy hotel on the beach or in a treehouse. As a child, I always wanted a treehouse because it signified "normalcy."

The dull white walls became a fresh canvas for the imagination. I often sprawled out on my bed and imagined beautiful things. Christmas lights and the smell of warm apple pie always made me feel cozy. I dreamt up the smell of sugary pastries. Since sugar was banned in the hospitals, I could only get the sweet stuff with my mind. I was a daydreamer. Sometimes I'd even notice the sides of my lips tighten and raise into a smile because of the wonderful emotions I created with my make-believe thoughts.

The crazy people who had scared me at first somehow became beautiful to me, perhaps because I related to them. They were real. They never masked their feelings or emotions, and they didn't care what others thought of them. They had stories like mine, hidden close to their hearts where no one could get to them.

The lady who decorated the bathroom in toilet paper was an "artist." She turned an otherwise unimaginative washroom into a fantastic place of mystery. Instead of cutting, like me, she strung toilet tissue. It was then I realized why a caged bird will sing. After a tragedy, you should be able to indulge in whatever sets your heart on fire.

Whatever makes you feel happy should be all you ever do.

The girl who sang awfully also provided entertainment. Even though her voice sounded like a wounded cat, there was a beauty about her passion. There is always a beauty about passion.

While I was in and out of the hospitals, I continued to work at the house with the girls. I usually timed my admittance around my workdays. It felt like I was going "home" for the weekend. Sure, it was a madhouse, but I understood chaos, and I functioned best in it.

Once I accepted that the hospitals were where I belonged, I started to fit in. Nobody was judged in the institutions; it was acceptable to act and feel however you wanted. For example, my wall obsession was not due to mere boredom. While I dragged my hand along the textured paint in the halls, I'd lose myself. It was possible to transport from the hospital to wherever I wanted through the simple touch of my fingertips to the wall. This was an adventure, and when I did it, I felt like a kid again.

When I didn't feel like a kid, I treated the others like the special girls I cared for. We colored pictures and then gave fake awards to the best artist. We watched a lot of movies, sometimes the same film over and over. The flame inside me stayed ignited by the thought that I would one day be able to tell my story and captivate audiences.

Once, while I gazed at the TV, flashes of my past fantasies of being a storyteller and an actress danced in my mind. Movies were my passion. When I thought of the dreams that made my heart sing, I became hopeful. I wondered if I'd ever be strong enough to leave the mental hospitals for good; I wondered if I'd have the ability to survive on my own.

But within the walls of the hospitals, I was sheltered. If the madman was real, he didn't know where I was. Even if he did, he would never be able to enter through the doors. The joint was built so that no one could escape, and I assumed that also meant it was difficult to get in, unless he came on a 5150, but that wasn't his style.

YET AGAIN, MY IMAGINATION SUGARCOATED the truth. The sight of the security guards reminded me that I was rich and famous. So rich and famous, I'd get bombarded if I ever left my giant mansion. So sought after, I had a stalker. My private chefs were on hand at all hours and prepared healthy food three times a day. My caretakers never offered me sugar because they cared too much—that's why they were called "caretakers." The colorful pills that I accepted with grace were flown in just for me; they were meant to heal my broken heart. The shower fairy always provided razors so I could shave my armpits and legs. She was also paid to French braid my hair every once in a while. The guards came in my room every hour when I slept to assure that no one had broken in and attempted to steal me or the shoe on my back.

The delusional mind I so often wished to silence had, yet again, saved my life. Eventually I would not be able to tell the difference between make-believe and actuality.

My boyfriend, Trevor

CHAPTER SEVENTEEN

A Beautiful Believer

The most powerful form of love is 'self-love.' Some people need
love from others in order to love themselves. When you love your-
self, you can easily love others, and you no longer require them to
validate you with their love.
From experience,
Jennifer Asbenson

It had been about a year since I told everyone I was kidnapped.
Since then, my life consisted of work and mental hospitals. When my
new evening shift ended, I drove straight home to my parents' house,
made something to eat, watched *Cops*, and went to bed. I rarely altered
from this self-set schedule. But Tyler's attempt to disrupt my routine
finally paid off when I accepted her invitation to a friend's house.

The home was a beautiful Spanish-style sanctuary. Large reddish
tiles led to two dark wood doors. The entrance sat behind a white
awning, with side curtains that tied to the stucco walls. *Is this the*
correct house? I wondered as I knocked.

Tyler answered the door and introduced me to her new man's
friend Trevor, who lived in the house with his mom. On this particular
night, Trevor's mother was elsewhere.

The entrance to the Palm Springs house was a mixture of cottage
and jungle. It was breathtaking: trees everywhere, grass patches, and
potent roses. Every part of me admired the luscious surroundings. My

treehouse would have fit perfectly in the yard of this home, blending in exquisitely.

Someone once told me that the first thing a woman does when she goes to the house of a potential suitor is to imagine if she could live there. Apparently, women have done this since the Dark Ages. During the first visit to Trevor's house, I didn't consciously wonder about this ancient practice. Looking back now, I see that I did.

Our eyes met. I pulled mine away and asked Tyler where the bathroom was. On the way, I explored the hall and the entrances of the rooms with my eyes only. Surely, the distractions would ease my nerves.

Trevor was tall, dark, and handsome. He was friendly, too, and very funny. One glance at him made me feel happiness again.

Throughout the night, Trevor gazed at me frequently. He insisted that in the white outfit I was wearing, I looked like an angel. He was not too shy to tell me this repeatedly.

Nervousness caused me to seek a few moments of refuge in the bathroom often. The linen-walled room was dimly lit by a cinnamon-scented candle. *Could it get any better?* I thought. The candle flame fluttered with the beat of my heart. The instant I had laid eyes on him, I was in love—proof I still had a heart.

After I pulled myself together in the bathroom, I looked in the mirror and pumped myself up with words of courage. The exhaust fan muffled my whispered madness.

"You look like a freakin' angel! An angel! Act normal. Just act normal." Then I took a deep breath, flushed the toilet, and returned to the living room. Trevor awaited my arrival with a huge, toothy smile.

"Are you having stomach issues or something?" he asked.

My face turned beet red. "Huh? Oh, no. No … Nooo. I'm okay."

He stood, as if to leave the room. "My mom has medicine. No big deal."

"No, I'm fine. Really. I was … just …" My finger pointed toward the bathroom. "I'm good."

He was silent for a second as he checked me out.

"Aren't you hot in that sweater?"

His thought switched. "Wanna run to the store to get some beers?"

If my dad had heard this, he would have said Trevor had diarrhea of the mouth. Trevor talked a lot, with a bunch of positive energy.

He did not demand an immediate answer.

"Oh. Beer?" I asked, confused. I looked over his shoulder to see Tyler and her boyfriend on the back patio; her boyfriend released a puff of smoke from his mouth. *Does Tyler smoke now?* I wondered.

The music played loudly on the stereo, nestled behind glass doors beneath the TV. Tall black speakers that displayed candles and framed family photos rattled throughout the living room. "Hotel California" was a smooth, familiar tune, but I had no idea who sang it. Trevor knew it too well. He rehearsed the lyrics and studied my face.

"Woo!" he yelled suddenly. His body seemed flimsy. My eyes focused on his every move.

He held an empty beer can in his hand. "The Eagles are the fuckin' best!" He squished the can with his lanky fingers. A nervous laugh could not be contained, although I tried to cover the sound with my hand.

"C'mon! Let's go!" He had a skip in his step as he exited through the open front doors. My head quickly drew back, and my eyes widened. I threw caution to the wind, grabbed my purse, and galloped beside him. *This is what a normal person would do,* I thought.

He hopped into a raised, shiny black Jeep Wrangler with no doors. "Do you have a car?" he asked as I got a running start to mimic him.

This was the perfect time to impress him. Not everyone our age had a car, and I knew mine was badass. "Ya, a little white one."

He began to pull out of the driveway and fiddled with the stereo. "Oh ya?"

He looked up and spotted the white Mazda RX-7. A look of surprise hit every inch of his face. His tongue was in the way as he spoke. "Whose car is—is that your car? Shut up!"

He parked the Jeep. "Let's take that!"

Trevor functioned at full throttle, which was good, because I was a snail. The balance this created between us was apparent.

Trevor rode shotgun as I drove my two-seater sports car. He continuously referred to the passenger seat as a shotgun. His enthusiasm made it funny.

A few blocks from his house, his excitement exploded. "Let's see how fast this baby can go! Let's live a little!"

I pointed at the liquor store. "Wait! Isn't this the store you wanted?"

"Ya!" He jumped out after the car was parked. I stayed in my car, mainly because I had horrible anxiety. And I usually walked differently around new people—I moved on the balls of my feet, like a nervous dancer. It was too soon in the relationship to show my insecurities. Instead, I sat and practiced cute expressions in the rearview mirror.

As I drove back to his house, I successfully steered the conversation off the car's speed potential. Trevor began to ask me a lot of personal questions. A fear surfaced from somewhere deep. *If he knew the real me, would he turn and run and never look back?*

Back at his house, we played cards and drank a lot of beer. The more I drank, the more I liked myself.

Even though Tyler had made many attempts to invite me to Trevor's, I was confused at why she didn't stress how fun the experience would be. She probably had, but I was too negative and into my own routine to imagine the best. People often pointed out how I overreacted to even the mildest circumstances, but this experience was way better than I could have imagined. I knew it would change my life.

Late at night, Tyler and her boyfriend separated from Trevor and me. Trevor swam in the pool in his backyard paradise and encouraged me to swim in my bra and underwear. At first, I hesitated, but then my tipsy brain reminded me that I had a nice figure. My pants, tank top, and sweater were flung onto the ground, and I jumped into the deep end.

When I returned to the surface, Trevor swam to me and held me like a sleeping baby. We began to kiss. In a sexy attempt to sweep hair out of my face, I exposed the cuts I had forgotten to hide. His eyes immediately averted. He was concerned.

"What the hell?"

His mouth opened, and he struggled to find his next words. "Are—what?"

I swam away and reached for my beer on the deck. "It's okay. I'm okay." After spotting the ladder, I climbed out of the pool and reached for my towel.

I pointed toward a structure across the backyard. "What's that?"

"What's what?" he asked.

A wooden, octagon-shaped gazebo hid behind the trees. I wobbled toward it. "What's in here?"

He climbed out of the pool and quickly toweled off. "The gazebo!"

Trevor ran barefoot down the dark path and met me inside. He flicked the striker on the lighter he quickly located. He adjusted the face of a small radio, wiping away the spiderwebs strewn across it. Music began to play as he searched for more unhidden webs and lit fire on them.

"So, did you try to kill yourself or something?" he asked.

A laugh unintentionally flew out of my mouth. "Me? No!"

We sat on his mom's massage table and shared a joint he pulled out of a drawer under the radio. He kept a lookout for spiderwebs and occasionally ripped into one with the squirmy flame. The marijuana convinced me to talk.

"Didn't Tyler tell you what happened to me?" I asked.

"No. What happened to you?"

He then became the jaw-dropped, one-person audience to my horror story. The entire time, he sat with his eyes wide and his mouth stiff.

My wrists were lit by the lighter. "These cuts here are from the twine."

The flame exposed my left forearm. "And the ones up here are where he cut me with the knife."

I lied to cover my self-inflicted wounds. He would never love me if he thought I didn't love myself, so I faked it.

He never sought out or burned down another web while I spoke. He believed me. His belief in my story lifted my spirits, so much so that I became excited about a shooting star. Of course, I made a wish for Trevor to love me.

"I'll kick that motherfucker's ass and rip his head off." His wild comments made me laugh.

"That stupid-ass, sick fuck! I'll show him!"

His sympathy and compassion wove stitches throughout my lacerated soul, and my cutting ended there.

When I wasn't in mental hospitals or at work, I was usually with Trevor or in regular hospitals. Even though I was significantly happier, I always thought I was sick. Hypochondriacs truly believe they are sick, even though they are fine, one doctor had assured me.

My health always worried me, and I often thought I was about to die. As I grew older, I began to realize I would not feel loved at the hospitals anymore like I did when I was a child. Sometimes a lost day would prove worth the trip to the emergency room, but usually not. The mental hospitals, on the other hand, guaranteed joy.

Trevor brightened my life and taught me how to live. His zest for life, his passion for the guitar, and his social skills made my wounded soul mend rapidly. But because I no longer knew how to regulate or limit myself, I'd soon be fighting for my life again.

There was always a lower level of lowness, and it always found me.

CHAPTER EIGHTEEN

It's Raining Nickels

My family and I had just returned from Laughlin where I had won one thousand nickels. Actual coins dropped out of the slot machines.

Most people would have traded the nickels for paper money, but not me. I wanted the coins. This was the first time I had ever won money. I had never seen so many nickels in my life, so I decided to keep them. The silver coins were shiny and pretty, and I enjoyed the *click* they made when I dropped them back onto themselves as they slipped through my fingers.

Once home, I put all the nickels in my little sports car. The glovebox, ashtray, and middle console were stuffed and all of the nooks and crannies too. If I showed Trevor all the nickels I won, he would be proud of me. The thought of us paying the Del Taco drive-through cashier with nickels amused me.

AFTER MEETING TREVOR, I MOVED into a small camper trailer on my parents' property. It was time for more privacy, and if the maniac did come to the house, he'd never find me.

A cord stretched from my parents' house to the trailer to relay electricity. After I straightened up my twinkle-lit hideout, I got ready to go to Trevor's.

The night was dark, and I was excited. As I drove, I remembered Trevor's voice when he asked me how fast the car went. The words *live a little* echoed through my head as if I were in a deep valley. *Finally, I feel alive*, I thought as I slowly began to accelerate.

The road had many twists and turns, but I had traveled it a million times before. A concrete divider ran down the middle to separate the opposing traffic.

My fears were abandoned; the power of my new, indestructible outlook on life reigned freely. My car zoomed by others, and the only evidence was a quick streak of light.

My inner pendulum swung one way or the other; it rarely idled. The medium between brave and afraid was hard to find. My decisions were quick and extreme. Freedom always seemed near.

Sometimes I felt sexy, and the test of my car's speed was one of those times. Rebellion flowed in my blood. Soul Asylum's "Runaway Train" played on repeat—my go-to song. The music blared as my hair blew in the wind. My lack of control appeared to be total control. Fully absorbed in the moment, I channeled my inner Sharon Stone from the movie *Basic Instinct*. She drove fast on curvy mountain roads because she was not one to fuck with.

Bright red flickers of light bolted from the front left side of my car. The sparks were fiery, like the flames that flutter away from a fire pit when roasting marshmallows. The flares became abundant.

Confused by the display, I wondered if the moment was fantasy or reality. Within seconds, a significant streak of sparks met my windshield like a blooming firework. A horrifying screech roared through the vehicle. At over eighty miles an hour, my car grazed the center concrete divider of the four-lane mountain grade.

In a panic, I rotated the steering wheel and collided with the mountain. In an instant, I was gone.

God causes us to pass out like that to protect us. If we stayed alert the entire time, we would not be able to process the information because it comes in too fast. Also, if we are out of it, it's easier to die and cross over.

When you experience psychological shock, you do not feel the physical damage to your body. You are in limbo. This happens in order to give God an opportunity to decide if it's your time or not. If it isn't, you wake up after the accident. If it is, you never wake up.

When I was passed out, I knew I was in limbo. I experienced some sort of dream—I felt like I was at the carnival on a tiny version of the ride Gravitron. The amusement ride looks like a UFO. You lean against the wall, the UFO spins, the floor drops out, and the UFO tilts. Because of its centrifugal force, people stay pressed against the walls. Like on the ride, my body and mind spun fast.

Silver, shiny stars erupted before my powerless eyes, and I witnessed a lengthy, brightened road and a compelling man. Nothing else—no pain, no thought, no regret, no worry, no dread. Only loud music, stars, a road, and a man existed.

Meanwhile, back in reality, the speed of the car, as it struck the mountain, caused it to flip numerous times and twirl out of control. A billion nickels danced in the air. Like a ragdoll, I drifted with the motions as the car tumbled southbound. My Mazda began to glide upside down. On its roof, it gracefully slid onward down the road, with no destination in mind. The manual sunroof detached, which allowed my head access to the blacktop. Part of my scalp was replaced with asphalt.

The car struck the center divider forcefully, came to a halt, and jolted me awake. In a catatonic trance, I attempted to evaluate the situation. The music seemed louder, and it occasionally skipped a beat. My eyes took a second to adjust to their new surroundings. The steering wheel pressed into my ribs, and blood rushed through my head. I dangled in a fetal position, trapped upside down in my mangled sports car. *This is not reality*, I thought. *Wake up!* But only my eyes and my mouth could move. Panic flooded my thoughts. It was then I realized I was claustrophobic.

Aware that the nightmare was real, I began to fear that another car would clobber me. The only view I had was through the scrunched window. As I hung overturned and helpless, headlights came toward my eyes. I screamed over the music and out to God. Because my left arm was elongated away from my body and trapped, my hands were unable to pray.

Unbeknownst to me at the time, a northbound "Bingo Bus" stopped when the driver and passengers discovered the crushed car. Some elderly folks on the bus felt certain that anyone in the car must be dead. The others, with faith, began to pray.

The headlights stopped. My eyes looked to the left, but the night was dark, and the lights blinded me. Between breaks in the music, voices yelled back and forth in the distance. I screamed internally, but tried to take deep breaths. The story of the song eased the torture.

The agony I endured came from the claustrophobia. At that moment in time, it was profound mind torture. In my experience with misery, I had imagined and debated many horrible deaths; death in a confined space moved to the top of the list. The anguish was insurmountable. Repetitive music alone could provoke insanity for some, but in my case, it was the only thing familiar and predictable. The music was my mind's saving grace.

The headlights were interrupted, and my left breast underwent rough manipulation.

"Arhhh," I said.

"You're alive?" a voice asked.

"That's my boob!" I yelled.

"Can you turn the music down?"

"No!" Pinned upside down, I hadn't bothered to reach for the stereo.

"She's still alive! Call 911!" the voice yelled.

"Help me!"

"Help is on the way," he said.

He began to ask me questions, but I could only answer with cries. Moments later, the paramedics and firefighters arrived. Again, I was asked and prodded to answer the same questions.

The "jaws of life" began to tear at the mangled passenger door. The apparatus was loud and intimidating. PTSD only made it worse. Images of a huge blade ravaging my body and blood splattering throughout the car debilitated me.

"Stop! Stop!" I yelled. The loud noise came to a pause. Only the music played. Since I felt out of touch and a bit insane, the song's lyrics persuaded me to push on. With sheer and utter confidence, I spoke again, "Hang on. I'm going to get out."

"No, Jennifer. Do not move. We will come to you."

Their demand was ignored.

With the unimaginable strength I had encountered and accessed once before, I began to expand every cell in my body. Metal began to crunch as I pried the aluminum coffin off me. Gently, I pulled my hand from its entrapment. In a skillful manner and with tremendous adrenaline, I busted the steering wheel away from me and began to crawl through the wreckage toward the passenger door. Each movement I made took pressure off my mind.

"Is she moving?"

"Jennifer, you will not be able to get out."

"Stay still. You are trapped."

The space was limited, but the cinder-block-sized gap to freedom failed to damper my will to succeed. Sideways, I shoved my head through the gap. The space was so small, it felt like the car was about to birth me.

"Pull my head," I said. I did not want to wait another second to break free from my metal imprisonment. As the belly-up car birthed me, my eyes began to glisten by what I saw next. Nickels all over the black asphalt road were illuminated by headlights and red emergency blinkers. They looked like silver stars. The loud music, the sight of the nickels, and the chaos enlightened me.

In emotional shock, I stood up and shook off. My arms were held by paramedics, and a gurney was placed under me. Their sense of urgency was memorable.

The car was in a disfigured mess. Its underbelly faced the sky. Its pose was similar to downward dog, a pose in yoga named after the way canines naturally stretch their entire bodies. The front of my Mazda was down and the back was up.

Traffic had ceased and backed up. The occupants of the cars picked up my nickels. It made me happy to see that the coins were saved. The nickels had a better story now.

Inside the ambulance, I noticed the skin on my hands had been replaced with glass and asphalt. My head began to burn, and when I touched the top of it, I felt asphalt and a large chunk of glass. The afflicted area was the size of a slice of toast. As I picked at it, I removed chunks of asphalt with long blond hair attached. The more I messed with it, the more my hair dislodged from my scalp. Once I removed the hair and road chunks, I felt bits of glass lodged into my scalp. The paramedics gave me a small plastic bag to put all of my damaged hair and scalp in, while I questioned them about the injuries.

"How did the road get in my head?" I asked.

"It looks like your head went out the sunroof," the paramedic said. "You're lucky to be alive. People in wrecks like yours don't normally survive."

My forehead began to pound. It was wet with blood and covered in glass and gravel. Like a monkey searching itself for ticks or fleas, I picked at my skin the entire trip to the emergency room.

At the hospital, X-rays revealed no broken bones. A male nurse scrubbed my wounds for hours with some sort of steel ball. The pain from the scrub was intolerable; it made me want to pass out. The entire time, I begged him to stop. Reluctantly, the nurse stopped and warned me that I still had glass and gravel inside my skin. He applied ointment to soothe the pain, and he wrapped the wounds.

In total, about twenty-five percent of my hair and scalp was lost in chunks. Forty percent of my forehead contained gravel and glass. Eighty percent of the skin on the back of my left hand was completely gone. And I had multiple cuts, scrapes, and bruises all over my body. Three teeth were also lost.

Five hours post-admittance, I was released. Trevor rushed to the hospital to pick me up. When he arrived, I was so excited. We were at the point in our relationship when our feelings were fresh, and we didn't know if the other person was really interested or not.

Trevor showed up with a smile on his face and flowers in hand. No one had ever given me flowers before, so I felt special. The flowers had a tiny card with them; I noticed it as we drove to his house.

As he sang along with "Sunshine on my Shoulders" on his stereo, I snuck a peek at the note. Trevor had written: *Jennifer, I'm so glad you are okay. I don't know what I would have done without you. I love you.*

Okay, it didn't actually say *I love you*. On the very bottom, in little letters, the card said *I (drawn heart) U*. He had drawn a heart to replace the word *love*. He also used a *U* instead of spelling out the word.

As I examined the words, I felt a surge of adrenaline rush through my veins. I gazed out the window and smiled and then looked back at the card to make sure I had read it correctly. I felt so loved, safe, and protected. When I saw how much Trevor cared about me, I surrendered all of my emotional fears. For the first time in my life, I felt true love. This feeling made me start to see the world differently. Everything I looked at was lovelier, and I was happier.

When we arrived at Trevor's house, his mom, Mariah, was there with open arms. Trevor and his mom cared for me. His mom was gentle and warm. She welcomed me to stay in their home while I healed.

MY PARENTS NEVER EVEN CAME to the hospital. A friend, who notified my mom while I was being treated, said my mom was more concerned about the car than me.

When I called my mom about the accident later that night, she told me that I was kicked out of the house. I wasn't welcome there anymore. She also said she heard about the accident from a friend who was on the Bingo Bus when it stopped. She said that some people on the bus figured the person in the car was dead, and others prayed. She didn't know how I always got so lucky, when I probably deserved to die due to carelessness.

WORK GAVE ME THREE WEEKS to heal. Severe whiplash and a swollen head made me look less than desirable as Trevor cared for me. The physical pain was worth the emotional gain, though, and the loss of the car was worth the love.

It is horrible to have physical pain and emotional pain at the same time. It is better when you only have one. I have endured both during my life enough to know that my choice would be physical pain over emotional distress anytime. If you feel cared for and loved, you heal faster and better, maybe because you have a reason to recover.

Nickels stayed scattered over the road for months to come. They were a constant reminder that it was not my time to die yet.

After about a month of healing, I returned to work. Right away, I noticed people treated me like I was fragile; they didn't get too close. Maybe they thought I was bad luck and they didn't want me to rub off on them.

Just days after my return, my manager approached me nervously. She told me she needed to speak to me. Awkward tension filled the air as I wondered what she had to say. Her body language told me she was uncomfortable. She took a deep breath, then exhaled her words.

"A rumor has been going around about you. It's not good."

"A rumor?" I asked. *After all I have been through, why would someone say something bad about me?* I thought.

Tears began to fill her eyes. "This is so hard."

I really liked my manager, so I tried to comfort her and tell her it was okay.

"I don't care! Nothing can be worse than everything I've already gone through. What is it?"

I stared at her with concerned eyes and a fake smile to ease her fear of my reaction.

She covered her face with her hands, then quickly withdrew them and blurted out her words.

"They say that you have AIDS!"

My Mazda RX-7 sports car before the crash

CHAPTER NINETEEN

Bottommost

Two years later, unemployed and in a daze, I clung to existence. In Trevor's bedroom, my hands began to ache. I lifted my fingers from the colored construction paper and stretched them out. Physical pain annoyed me—unless I was in search of attention—so I had to rid myself of it. In the bathroom, I opened the medicine cabinet and discovered some powerful pain medication.

With cupped hands, I drank the sink water to wash the pills down. My face began to agitate me, so I splashed cold water on my skin and rubbed my worn-out eyes. As I lifted my head to look in the mirror, I began to tremble. My odd reflection drew me closer to the mirror, and I focused in on my eyes. Unlike eyes that reveal a soul, mine were vacant—completely void. My empty eyes spoke volumes. They were gloomy. In the darkness, I felt cold. The future could not be seen, only the present and past, and neither proved good. My eyes stayed riveted to the mirror until my attention was averted elsewhere.

My kooky lips engrossed me. They were a part of my face but suddenly seemed unfamiliar. My curiosity forced me to open my mouth wide, and what I witnessed was heinous.

My tongue flopped around uncontrollably, like a fleshy fish out of water with no head or tail. The bizarre display startled me. With a firm pinch from my fingers, I tried to calm the freakish mouth assault.

As I wrestled my tongue, a bright idea popped into my mind. *An icy cold beer sounds good. I wonder if we have any left.*

Sidetracked, my outrageous behavior ceased. I headed for the kitchen, grabbed a beer, and returned to the bedroom.

As I cracked the beer open, I examined my craft space on the floor and jumped back to work. With serious focus, I stretched out on the floor and concentrated fully.

Multi-colored construction paper, cut into index-card-sized rectangles, covered the planked hardwood floor. Neon markers were scattered about. Eighty handmade business cards patiently sat in stacks of twenty as I attempted to reach my goal of one hundred. Each card was different and unique—some contained art or stickers and others were simpler. Every card had a new font, but the messages read the same.

The business cards were made to help me find a new job caring for people with disabilities. My job title was written out on the top with my phone number under it. My plan was to hand them out and leave them in mailboxes, with the hope that someone would need my help.

Anytime Trevor walked by, I covered my project. We weren't supposed to show each other our creations until we were finished. He interrupted his multimedia art creation to offer me a puff of his joint, but I declined because I didn't smoke that stuff.

A couple hours later, I finished my business cards. My excitement was obvious. After I stood, I clapped my hands and did a quick dance in place. Then I stretched my tight fingers.

"Okay. I'm done. Close your eyes," I said.

With a paintbrush in one hand, he stopped in his tracks and shut his eyes.

"Hold out your hand."

Excited, he put his hand out and faced his palm upward. I placed a small stack of business cards in his hand.

My fingers wiggled wildly with excitement.

"You can look."

He opened his eyes and drew the cards closer. He began to laugh as he glanced through the stack.

"Business cards!" He flipped one over to find it blank on the back. "These are badass."

"Yes!"

He laughed loudly as he mouthed the words on the cards to himself.

"Good idea! If you say you are disabled, people will hire you because they will feel bad for you!" He tried to high-five me, but I was confused.

"What? No! What do you mean?" I asked.

"Your cards say that you are a disabled caretaker."

"No! I'm a caretaker for the disabled. That's why I wrote *Disabled Caretaker*!" I began to get paranoid that he didn't understand.

"As I read the card, it appears that *you* are disabled." He took a hit off the joint.

"Ahhhh!"

After I screamed at the top of my lungs into a dingy pillow, I cried and laughed as I ripped my hours of work into little pieces and threw them into the air like confetti. When every card was shredded, I grabbed the joint, breathed in deep, and sighed in frustration.

It was six o'clock in the morning. We had been up for two days. Our blood had been poisoned and could have contained battery acid, drain cleaner, lantern fuel, and antifreeze. We didn't know, and we didn't care. We were high on methamphetamine.

FOR A FEW MONTHS, WE did "speed" often and never left each other's sides. Trevor hadn't invited me to live at the house, but I somehow moved myself in. We had oodles of fun, and I loved my new carefree, rebellious lifestyle.

Trevor had such a zest for life. He partied every day and held a job on the side. He didn't care about what others thought of him or us, and I loved that. He was a free spirit, and I was a loon. We meant the world to each other.

Once, we had sex in a random cave that we stumbled upon in the desert. The date was not as romantic as it might sound. A stampede of annoyed bats interrupted our sexy escapade and forced us to flee in terror.

Who knew there were caves in the desert? Trevor had been the expert on all the cool spots to have a good time. It never crossed my mind until now that I might not have been the first girl he brought to the rustic love dungeon.

Trevor and I could find excitement anywhere. We were never bored. For fun, we went on adventures in his Jeep. We plowed through streams and climbed daunting hills. There were no feats the sturdy four-wheel drive couldn't conquer.

When Trevor's mom was away from the house, we had pool parties and invited people over. We had barbecues in the backyard with Tyler and her boyfriend. The guys would jump off the roof into the pool as Tyler and I covered our eyes and clenched our teeth. Their dangerous behavior secretly exhilarated us small-town girls.

As I stare at the backyard pool from my treehouse, I see vivid images of Trevor. He was always by the pool with a smile on his face. If he wasn't skimming for leaves, he was dancing with a margarita in his hand. He exuded happiness and positivity.

When we first met, Trevor was on break from his third year at San Diego State University, where he majored in criminal justice. He once told me that he came to visit his mom and got "stuck" in the desert. While we were dating, he worked as a waiter at a high-end restaurant and dabbled in artistic affairs.

For selfish reasons, I never encouraged Trevor to return to college. If I knew he would die of cirrhosis of the liver at age thirty-three, I'd like to think I would have used all my power to convince him to return to finish his degree. On the other hand, if he had returned, this story would lose significant beauty and someone else would have never entered my life. This is where I see things happen as they are supposed to, and that everything is meant to be.

My employment never lasted for more than a month at a time. PTSD caused me to no longer think clearly. Constant thoughts of being murdered at work turned me into a panicky whack job. When I was a waitress, the images disturbed me so much that I'd tremble and drop plates. When I picked them up, I'd stutter and shudder.

My warped mind propelled simple gestures into a dreadful strato-sphere. The chef polishing his knife had a secret plan to butcher me. The guy mopping the floor was most likely his accomplice.

I disappeared on the job often. If I didn't sit on the toilet and convince myself to breathe, I would sit there and use my knees as a desk to write notes. At least once a week, I wrote a note to either my boss or a trusted co-worker revealing my killer. If I were to suddenly go missing, the notes blatantly identified my killers. The waitress order slips would help detectives locate my body faster, before it decomposed.

Needless to say, I felt a remarkable sense of relief after I quit a job. The two rituals that followed the release of responsibility were always consistent. First, I'd hyperventilate. Then I'd take a bath. Man, did I look forward to those baths.

Water had always represented comfort to me. Sometimes I secretly called it Mom. In the warm bath, with no presence of light, I escaped to a kingdom of solace, a place where shower water rained for hours onto my face while I curled up into the collective puddle below. The retreat of the bath was a place where tears could freely add to the level of my fluid submersion. In that place, I felt understood by the water.

My life took a turn for the worse after I quit my first job at the house with the girls two years earlier. I missed the girls daily, but I did not plan to return. When my manager revealed who had spread the vicious AIDS rumor, I lost my mind completely. Trevor's love alone did not hold the power to save me from my own demons.

My job in the home for the girls was the last string in my life that held me together, gave me hope, and made me feel proud. When the string was cut, I felt like a punctured balloon with an unchosen purpose to violently strike walls, lose steam, and plummet from existence.

After my car accident, three words had brought me back to life. Now four words destroyed me.

"It was your mom," my manager said.

The words were heavy. Her lips were reluctant. I noticed all the curves and creases around her mouth. It felt like I was stuck in quicksand; I could only continue to stare as she sat in silence.

Maybe that was the only way my brain could comprehend the words—with an intense slowness. When they sunk in, warm blood flushed my face. Anger and sadness, equally strong, combined on my face, causing a well of tears to brew. As I tried to hold the feelings back, my gut began to ache, and I wondered if I might vomit. A sudden forced smile induced a cascade of tears.

With downturned lips and weakened body language, my manager set her hand on my shoulder.

"Your mom was fired," she said.

My eyes wandered the blank walls as I flashed back to the treatment I received at work, prior to the conversation. People had walked around me as if I had cooties.

The reason for the awkwardness at work was now clear. My lips quivered as I lifted my finger in an attempt to reveal my thoughts. Weakly, I stood, grabbed my purse, and took off out the front door. On my way out, I told my manager I would be back, but I never returned. Instead, I went to the store, bought alcohol, and returned to Trevor's house.

In a perturbed drunken stupor, with the bedroom wall as my support, I phoned my mom. My anger could be heard through my breath.

"Why would you tell everyone that I have AIDS? Are you fucking crazy?"

"Because you were raped," my mom answered.

My anger could not be controlled. "That … was … my … job!"

"Jennifer, usually when people are raped, they get AIDS."

"That's not true! I wasn't even raped!"

"That *was* your job, you said? Did you get fired too?"

"No! Why did you tell people that I have AIDS?"

There was silence.

"Sorry, that's what I thought."

Confused, I didn't know whether to believe her or not. It would comfort me to view her as ignorant, but I began to wonder if her claim could be true. AIDS was spread through sex, I knew that. The inebriation didn't help me sort my thoughts. Out of frustration, I threw the phone across the room, and my back slid down the wall until I reached the floor.

The images of the attack played in my head, and I reminded myself that penetration never happened. *But did it?* I wondered. *He did bite me. Could that have given me AIDS?*

But I no longer cared. My self-worth was disputed, and my downward spiral was set into motion.

As I sit here and write this from the safety of my treehouse, my mind is boggled. Why would my own mother start a rumor like that? Maybe she told people I had AIDS so they would feel bad for her and show her sympathy. Maybe she truly believed that if a person was raped, they would get AIDS. Or maybe she was cruel and saw that I was indestructible, so she made it her life's mission to try and destroy me. Like a party candle you can't blow out, I have never failed to reignite.

Some nights, I would lie in the middle of the road, look at the sky, and talk to God. Even though Trevor loved me, I was lost. Drugs and alcohol made everything worse. Fights between us erupted like volca-noes. We'd make up, but fight again. It became a vicious cycle, until we finally broke up.

AT MY LOWEST, I MOVED back into my parents' house. Unloved, desperate, and vulnerable, I attracted chaos. I was a magnet for the undesirables. And I began to feel suicidal. If I didn't get to a hospital, I knew I would kill myself.

In the emergency room, I stood agitated. At the admittance window, an attendant assisted a man with a bloody leg.

With a sense of urgency, I interrupted, "I need help." It was clear I had had a rough night.

In a bossy attempt to teach me manners, the woman stood and pointed at my chest. "One moment, ma'am. You need to take a seat. We will be with you in just a minute."

Normally I cared what others thought, but the horrific images of self-destruction controlled my mind.

"I'll be dead by then!" I yelled.

All eyes were on me. The waiting room filled with gasps, and parents pulled their children close to shelter them. The nurses lifted their heads, but no one took action, so I headed to the doors that led outside.

"I'm going to kill myself!" I yelled.

Unable to stop the destructive momentum, I walked through the parking lot with haste. The street in front of me, with a steady flow of traffic, became my target. A semi-truck in the back of traffic caught my eye, so I sped up to assure I would meet it in time.

Shoes hit the pavement behind me, accompanied by loud, out-of-shape breaths. Like a prisoner on the run, I never looked back. I began to sprint. As the truck entered my vicinity, I thrust myself in front of it. The truck driver slammed on his brakes and swerved. I was tackled to the ground by hospital employees. Because I knew what would happen next, I became combative. A sharp stick in my thigh rendered me helpless.

My eyes rolled back in my head. As I turned off, I knew I was in good hands, and I knew where I would wake up. One thing I did not know was that this time, my life would forever be changed in the mental hospital.

My daughter Augusta's drawing which, for me, symbolizes hope

CHAPTER TWENTY

The Black Angel

Up and down the halls, I danced and laughed and skipped blissfully. This place was where I felt comfort. It was my home.

Soon I found my favorite chair—perfectly placed against the wall—and sat down to watch the others. *The most interesting people in the world are the ones who don't care about what others think. Maybe one day I will be like them*, I thought.

The morning medications had not yet delivered me to the puppet state I craved. So instead of defaulting into my fantasy world, I adopted the world around me.

An older woman walked through the room and spoke to herself. Drool fell from her mouth as she scratched at her private area. Naturally, I averted my eyes to find someone less gross. A woman rocked back and forth on a couch with her hands in the prayer position. She repeated the word *no* over and over. Annoyed by the unsettled emotions I developed, I looked away again. My attention was drawn to a man who yelled violently for medication. He pounded the thick glass window with his hand, and then hit the glass with his head.

Imagine a visit to your family. When you arrive, you find everyone in a bad mood or sick. Perhaps your sister broke up with her boyfriend, and your brother is on the run from the police. The scene before you is shocking because what you had imagined in your mind, before you arrived, is very different. Your expectations now cause you pain in the form of disappointment. That is how I felt as I sat in my favorite chair in the hospital many years ago.

The grief I experienced was far from pleasant. My once-present smile was lost. With trembling lips, my eyes filled with moisture. Blood rushed to my face. My eyes wandered the floor as I searched for any trace of beauty. With my head low, I didn't lift my eyes because I feared I'd witness more anguish.

In the old hard chair, I sat with my legs crossed and my back slouched over. My hands held the opposite elbow on my lap.

Accidentally, my eyes met another's. I looked into my lap. For comfort, I began to mimic the woman lost in prayer. In silence, I rocked back and forth as I wondered if the eyes that recently caught mine were still on the prowl.

I SOUGHT THE SOLACE OF the mental hospital anytime I couldn't deal with the outside world, but this time was different. My arrival offered no peace. The feelings I had, before I came in, did not go away. A desire to rebel against the whole world controlled my thoughts. For some reason, I couldn't shake the agitation that built up inside me.

The grim thoughts will cease once the medications kick in, I assured myself.

In an attempt to avoid the man with the eyes, I stood with my back hunched over and faced my chair toward the front entrance. My head was raised just enough for my eyes to view the hands on the clock.

The sooner the medications kicked in, the better. As I studied the large white clock, I felt trapped in my own head. Not allowed to look elsewhere, I tried to force happy thoughts.

Everything happens for a reason, I thought. *Everyone has a purpose.* I reminded myself to feel better about what I had witnessed. But my thoughts just irritated me more, and I wondered if I was even given the correct medication.

The medications they usually gave me blocked my emotional receptors. At inappropriate times, the pills caused me to become happy or sad or angry, but not for long. The most important side effect was numbness to emotional pain.

In the mental hospitals, I never knew what medications they gave me. My diagnoses included depression, anxiety, bipolar disorder, OCD, ADHD, schizophrenia, borderline personality disorder, and dependent personality disorder. On top of all the regular medications, I was also given medication to control the horrible side effects of the initial prescription drugs.

Twenty painful minutes after I fixated on the clock, my thoughts improved. My anxiety calmed down, and I had a strong desire to move around. No longer annoyed by the man who was staring, I walked to a long table and sat across from him. He looked nice; he had a round face, a shiny black head, and warm, dark eyes. He appeared to be trustworthy.

He sat in the same spot often. On previous visits I noticed him but never spoke to him. He was some sort of employee but not a nurse; he dressed in normal clothes. Perhaps he was an undercover security guard or a professional observer of patients. He definitely was not a patient; he acted too responsible, respectful, and kind. Anytime he was around, I felt safe.

My eyes met his often. I almost felt like he knew something good and true about me, but it was our secret. I leaned into him as if he were a friend. At first, he pretended not to notice me.

"You don't belong here," he said.

Immediately, I jumped up. "Oh, sorry!"

He laughed. "No wait! You can *sit* here. I'm sayin' ya don't belong *here*, in this place."

Surprised by his random comment, my forehead crinkled. "Oh, why?"

"Trust me," he said.

He monitored the room as if we were secret thieves, preparing for a heist. He sat sideways on the bench and never spoke directly to me.

"Somethin' bad happened to ya, but you're strong. I watch ya."

To hide my emotions, I cracked a joke. "You watch me? That's kinda creepy."

He smiled. "Ya know what I mean." He let out an exhausted sigh. "Do you wanna live here the rest of yer life?"

Nobody had ever asked me that, and it made me want to yell no. On the other hand, I thought I'd miss the place.

"No … I guess …"

He abruptly interrupted. "You don't."

His no-nonsense response made me quiet for a few seconds. In the silence, I examined my chewed fingernails.

"How do you know what happened to me?" I asked.

"I just know."

He repositioned himself so that I got a better view of his back. He placed his elbows on the table. His legs were stretched and folded in front of him. A bit more relaxed, he turned his head when he spoke. I could view either his right or left eye, but never both.

"I've been here long enough to know these things. I also see that ya keep comin' back."

My teeth bit what was left of my nails as I pretended not to listen. The guilt I felt was that of a girl who was caught with her hand in the cookie jar.

He was not done with his speech. "I've seen people come in here often and stay for years. That's not livin'. You don't want to be here."

For some reason, his words ignited a flicker of inspiration. To avoid personal responsibility, I attempted to defend myself. "I get stuck here because of the medication."

His still mouth convinced me to continue.

"They admit me and give me *so many* meds; I turn into a zombie and end up staying a while. It's not my fault."

The man slowly nodded his head as if he agreed with me.

"Do you want to be a zombie the rest of yer life?"

My eyes reverted to the itchy-crotch woman. Her presence knocked the wind from me as I imagined myself to be her in the future. I gulped for air.

"No."

"Then ya need to figure out how to stop takin' them."

"You have to take the meds. The nurses check your mouth after they give them to you."

He shook his head.

"They don't check everyone's mouth," he said.

My eyes widened, and I wondered if he was really a patient who found it fun to mess with my fragile mind.

"Whose mouth don't they check?" I asked.

He pointed his fingers to his eyes and then at the other patients. "Watch, and you will see," he whispered.

A FEW DAYS WENT BY, and I continued to take my pills like clockwork. The clues were harder to figure out when I was loaded. When medication time came, I watched the nurses check all the patients' mouths. Confused and convinced that the man had misinformed me, I sought him out.

The man was in his usual spot. He noticed me sitting behind him.

"They check *everyone's* mouth," I said.

"Watch closer."

The entire day, I watched like a hawk. The routine was precise and always the same. The "med freaks" received their medication first because they begged for it all day long. Then the nurses administered meds to everyone else. *What am I not seeing?* I wondered.

That night, I lay on my bed for hours and zoned in on the ceiling as I thought about the medication situation. The process played in my mind so frequently it became hypnotic. Like an image of sheep jumping over a fence, I pictured patient after patient opening their mouths, one after another. Eventually, the continuous rhythm put me to sleep on my back, where I never slept.

Startled by my awkward position in bed, I woke in the middle of the night and sat straight up. Immediately, an epiphany followed. *The med freaks!* I thought. *They never check the med freaks because the nurses know they are taking the pills, and they want them out of the way.* It was then I knew my acting skills would come into play. After I returned to my normal sleeping position, I hurried back to sleep because I knew my performance would start the next day.

When I woke at six in the morning, I began to beg for the medication. Like I had witnessed in my earlier observations, the requests were denied. Med time was at eight o'clock, I was told, and I would receive my meds then. This gave me more time to convince them I was jonesing it.

"Is it med time yet?" I'd ask every twenty minutes for the next two hours.

At seven o'clock, breakfast was served. Like a bird, I picked at my food and continued to look at the med window as if I might miss their call.

At seven thirty, I stood by the pill delivery window. The usual med freaks swarmed around me. Casually, I mimicked their agitated behavior.

Behind the window, the pills were arranged in small white paper cups. The nurse observed and noted the other three patients and me, pacing before her. No nurses stood outside the window near us, like usual. She leaned forward to open the window, and I jumped in front of her face.

With her mind elsewhere, she handed me my meds. With desperation, I thanked her and threw the pills back into my mouth. As I skipped away, I threw the crumpled cup into the trash. Within a minute, the nurse yelled out that it was med time, and other nurses began to organize the remaining patients in single file. *This is the perfect opportunity for me to disappear,* I thought.

In my room, I spit the pills into the toilet and flushed it. In the swirls of the toilet water, I saw hope.

When the man I now viewed as "the Black Angel" arrived, I joyfully pranced up behind him and sat on my knees. I tapped him on the back. He smiled.

"You finally figured it out," he said, as if he had been confident I would.

My face was lit with glee. "Yep."

"Good. Now whatever you do, don't flush 'em."

"What? Why?"

"Just don't."

"Okay."

Now confused about what to do with the pills, my mind wandered. As I stood, he stopped me.

"Wait. When you get sick, just say you have the flu."

"Sick?"

"Withdrawals."

In my room, I searched for another place to hide the pills. The thought of getting sick made me have second thoughts about my new medication plan. But I had someone to impress, someone who made me believe I had a reason to live.

In my small cabinet closet, I found my little mountain of feminine napkins. The pink-wrapped pads were given to me by a nurse who had asked what I used for my monthly periods. This was the same nurse who passed out toothpaste, shampoo, hair combs, and other personal care products. One day, after she had handed me soap, she confronted me.

"Uh, honey. What are you usin' to take care of your feminine needs?" she asked.

Confused by her question, I raised the soap in the air. "Soap?"

"Soap! You better not be up to somethin' fishy." She reached into a secret bag on her cart and pulled out a large handful of pink feminine napkins.

"Here, these should last you a while."

She shook her head and looked annoyed as I walked off.

Perhaps she thought I used a sock or a banana peel as a pad. The fact of the matter was, I used neither. Periods never came for me. *Amenorrhea* was what one gynecologist called it. Because I didn't have a monthly period, I would never be able to get pregnant, he told me. There would be no blood to feed the baby.

Before I stuffed my tiny trophies into the pads, I examined them. The pad is meant to stick to underwear. After I removed the strip of thin paper to reveal the sticky area, I made a tiny hole through the adhesive and pulled out little chunks of cotton. The cotton was messy, and particles of it suspended briefly in the air. After I inserted the medication, I would stick the pad in my underwear and carry on about my day.

Five pills a day were hidden in the pad. When the pad became worn out, I'd swap it with a fresh, sturdy new one.

My new responsibility gave me a sense of purpose and control. Whenever I would transfer the pills to a new pad at night, I would first study, organize, and count them. They made me feel proud. A bit of encouragement, accompanied with a secret task, gave me a new lease on life. The only downfall was that the larger my collection grew, the sicker I got.

The withdrawals were intolerable and made me second-guess my efforts. My head pounded constantly, and I experienced exhaustive night terrors. After I had a nightmare, I would toss and turn. In the morning, I'd vomit.

After a few days, my mind began to see things more clearly. A fake cough and body aches were added to my symptoms to hide the withdrawal evidence.

Day after day, the Black Angel encouraged me to push on. He assured me that the withdrawals would soon stop.

Before I could leave, I had to speak with the weekly discharge psychologist. I answered all the questions correctly and was released.

After I packed my belongings—mostly pads, shampoo, tissue boxes, and toothpaste—I smiled and said good-bye to the Black Angel. He finally made eye contact and smiled back.

"You take care of yourself now, ya hear."

"Okay," I replied as I walked out the self-locking door.

"Hey! I never want to see you again!"

Seven days and thirty-five crotch-crushed pills later, I waddled out of the mental hospital.

Trevor was the only person who could pick me up. Even though we were no longer together, I was excited to see him. As he drove down the freeway, I told him I had a surprise. I reached into my pants and pulled out the large puffy feminine napkin.

When Trevor was able to comprehend my actions, he pulled his body away from me.

"Eww! What the fuck? Are you crazy?"

"Nope, just the opposite."

The multi-colored pills were exposed as I tore open the pad.

"I hid all of my medications! That's how I got out," I said.

"That is so gross. Get rid of it!"

"That's littering!" I yelled.

The pills were thrust out the window. A few tried to cling to the pad's cotton inner lining, but a violent shake helped them take the leap. We left them scattered on the freeway, powerless. As we drove, I hoped the pills would be crushed by hot tires and never have the ability to alter anyone's fragile mind again.

A WEEK LATER AT MY parents' house, I continued the withdrawals. Alice bought me a pregnancy test, which I refused to use at first, because I knew I couldn't get pregnant. According to her, all of my symptoms seemed related to pregnancy. The last straw was the night I woke up at two in the morning and hyperventilated as I begged for strawberry ice cream.

"You're crazy to wake us up in the middle of the night for ice cream!" she yelled. Then she went back to bed.

One day, when no one was home, I decided to do the test. As I peed on it, two lines immediately showed up. Just like that, at the same time. Two lines meant I was pregnant. My heart stopped. My hand grasped the white stick tightly. *I'm never going to a mental hospital again*, I thought as I cried with the most joy I had ever felt in my life.

THE OBSTETRICIAN WAS SHOCKED I had gone three months without knowing I was pregnant. My pregnancy would be shorter than most, he said, since I only had six months to go.

After those six months, I delivered a beautiful baby girl. Within a few moments, I was told that she was disabled.

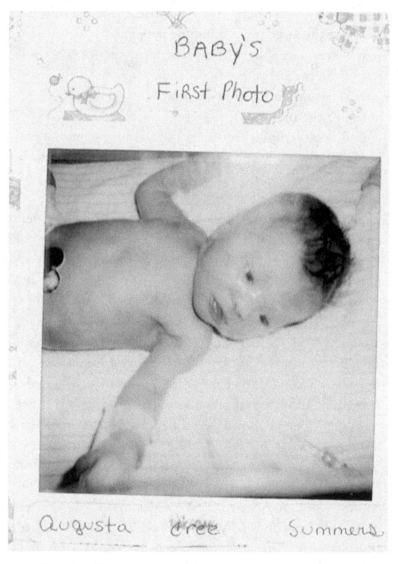

The photo I was left with before my baby was taken away

CHAPTER TWENTY-ONE

Augusta

When I was pregnant, I was the happiest girl in the world. Sure, I was single, had no job or car, and lived with my parents, but I was happy. Welfare paid me four hundred dollars a month, and I received food stamps and got on a program that gave me free healthy food, like milk and eggs and cheese.

Right away, I developed my plan to be a great mom. For me, it was easy—I would just do the opposite of what my mom did. All of my unhealthy habits were replaced with good ones. When I was pregnant, I did not drink alcohol or do drugs of any kind, not even medication. If people smoked near me, I would become upset and move, because I didn't want people to force my unborn baby to breathe secondhand smoke. My baby would be healthy, no matter what.

All of the bad stories of my life were pushed far out of my mind. My greatest fear was that the state would take my baby away if someone thought I was an unfit mother. I would prove to be very capable.

The upstairs room I had lived in as a teen was all mine when I was pregnant. For hours, I would obsess with the cleanliness and perfection of the room. A clear path was formed from the bedroom to the bathroom so that I wouldn't fall and smash my baby in an avalanche of random crap my mom had stockpiled outside my door.

My room was beautifully decorated. A crisp white and light blue bassinet sat in the corner. The little bed was from a secondhand baby store and had only been used once. Stuffed animals from the fifty-cent claw machine at the bowling alley were positioned around the inside, and a pink embroidered blanket—a gift from a sweet, elderly bingo player—draped over the edge.

No one was allowed in the room for any reason. If I heard anyone come up the stairs, I would ask who it was and question their business. It was usually a dog or cat—immediately scolded away—but rarely a human. No person or animal would ever intrude on my overly protected nest.

WHILE PREGNANT, I STUDIED AT home with books from a local Christian school and received my GED. Whenever I had a chance, I read. Sure, they were children's picture books, but that didn't matter. I wanted my daughter to think I was smart. Naturally, I read them over and over so that I would sound like a good reader. When I read, I became animated, and one day my mom heard me and yelled out, "Who are you talking to up there?" Because I was embarrassed, I didn't read aloud again for several years.

When I told my mom I was pregnant, she instantly treated me with unexpected kindness. If I had known she would be *Alice* throughout my entire pregnancy, I probably would have gotten pregnant when I was twelve. At the time, her sweetness prompted a yearning to have a second baby. But I only ever had one child.

Alice and I would go to the bowling alley on Wednesdays. She was in a bowling league and was quite good, even though she had bursitis in her fingers. Bursitis was painful and was probably another curse from God, she said. No matter how bad the pain, we never missed our weekly trip to the bowling alley and to bingo. Both sports required the use of her hands, but the fun always replaced the pain. Once, I even convinced her to play darts with me. Another time we played Pac-Man, and she would scream with angst any time the ghosts in the dotted maze got near her. Whoever invented the game was insane, she said, because in real life there would only be *one* scary ghost, not *four*.

Anytime her hands failed her, she blamed the bursitis. She told me she could no longer grasp things. In her defense, her fingers appeared to be damaged—knobby in areas that should have been straight and swollen in parts that should have been smaller.

Her fingers demanded my attention too frequently. Most of the time, they triggered my anxiety. Her witch-like fingers twitched and lifted off the steering wheel as she drove. She insisted she couldn't control it, but I thought it was all for show. After bowling, we would go to the humane society to play bingo. To my surprise, her fingers never lifted off the handheld bingo dauber.

We sometimes went to thrift stores and picked out cute, baby girl clothes. Before the doctor even told me, I knew I would have a girl. I could just feel it. I also prayed at night to remind God that I wished for a girl.

MY FAVORITE PAIR OF PREGNANCY sweatpants revealed the baby's name. The label caught my eye one day, and I imagined a sweet little blond girl with an angelic face. I spoke to her throughout my pregnancy, calling her by name, *Augusta*, before she was even born. It was a sign, I knew, because labels had never spoken to me before.

Alice, on the other hand, paid close attention to brand names. At the thrift stores, she would hold up ordinary clothes and yell to me, "Jennifer! This would look nice on you!"

As my hands cradled my belly, I'd slowly look up with intentionally crossed eyes. The clothes she chose were always outdated or for old ladies. If I said I didn't like them, she murmured to herself and searched for the tag with haste. Then she would make an announcement to get my attention.

"But it's expensive!"

She usually struggled to pronounce the names. She figured if I had never heard of it, it must be expensive. Sometimes, just to humor her, I pretended to like a shirt or dress she selected. When we placed our items on the counter to check out, I would hide a few clothing pieces somewhere and pray she wouldn't see them. To my relief, she never did.

Alice and I had a lot of fun together when I was pregnant. Because my guard was down, I began to reveal my sense of humor. My silly antics made her laugh uncontrollably. One time, I mimicked another player at bingo and caused my mom to pee her pants. She immediately sent me to the thrift store to buy her dry bottoms.

Her laughter and happiness made me feel special. It was uncommon to see her like this. I had waited my whole life to have my mom *feel* like my mom, so I relished every minute.

WHILE I WAS PREGNANT, I occasionally visited Trevor. The thought that my daughter should have a father made me gravitate toward him. It became a problem that I no longer drank and he did. He was carefree. He acted like every day was his last. People loved him for that. He didn't seem out of control, but I felt our baby deserved a sober dad.

Trevor was excited about my pregnancy and would tell everyone that I was pregnant. He rubbed and kissed my belly and treated me like I was physically disabled, which I loved. Trevor wanted to be involved with every aspect of the pregnancy. He even chose the baby's middle name, Cree. *Cree is a beautiful middle name*, I thought. *Augusta Cree Summers.*

The burning sage in my treehouse reminds me of a discovery I made after my daughter was born. Not long after her birth, I found out that Cree was the name of one of Trevor's ex-girlfriends. Trevor's last name was Summers. Augusta Cree Summers became the baby's legal name. But when I found out that Trevor pulled a fast one on me, I wanted to change her middle name to Sage. *Augusta Sage Summers.* When I realized her initials would be A.S.S., I decided to keep Cree.

Fantasies of the baby's arrival and our life together consumed my thoughts. She would be my best friend. She would also be beautiful, smart, and popular. And she would own a million pretty dresses. Most of all, she would be loved. We would always be there for each other, and I would never feel alone again.

AUGUSTA'S DELIVERY DATE WAS CIRCLED on my calendar with a bright pink marker. My labor induction was set for three o'clock in the afternoon on Friday, May 17. The baby never dropped, and I was a week overdue, so I had to set an appointment to have her.

When Friday finally came, I was nervous. A bond had developed between my unborn baby, my belly, and me. I loved being pregnant. During my pregnancy, people did not judge me; they automatically liked me and treated me kindly. For nine months, I felt complete. And although I would have a brand-new baby, I knew I would miss the consistency of the pregnancy and all of its perks. When I walked into the hospital, I mourned the end of pregnant life.

The delivery room had five people present: the doctor, my mom, Trevor, his mom, and the nurse. Augusta Cree Summers arrived early in the morning on Saturday, May 18, 1996. Her birth was so magical that I cried.

When the baby was born, they placed her on my chest. She was beautiful. She had bloody, dark brown hair and large blue eyes. As she screamed, she held onto her hands and thrust her arms out. She was so new, and her fragility stunned me. The nurses cleaned her and wrapped her and gave her back to me. They helped me try to breastfeed her, but she wasn't able. Her lungs began to gurgle. The doctor told me that the baby needed to be checked over in the ICU because he didn't like how her lungs sounded. And then, my baby was taken away from me.

After I demanded that my family leave the room to seek answers, I begged God not to let her die. Shortly after, my mom re-entered the room with a sad look on her face.

My face grew red with fury. "What?"

"Don't get mad at *me*," she said as she looked around the room for occupants. She stood near my left shoulder and stared down at me. "If

I could do it, so can you."

My teeth grit together tightly, and my fists clenched shut. "What are you talking about?"

My mom lowered her voice. "The baby is handicapped. She's like Jay Jay. Everything will be okay."

My eyes did not blink, and my nostrils started to flair like a bull before it charges.

She was a liar, and I knew it.

To gain deliverance from her psychological torture, I screamed at the top of my lungs. The nurse rushed into the room, followed by the doctor, Trevor, and his mom.

As I pointed at the emotional intruder, I lost it.

"She said my baby is handicapped—that she's disabled!"

The room grew silent, so I elaborated.

"That is what she said! She came in here and told me that my baby is handicapped."

Everyone was shocked. My mom just stood there as if she had done nothing wrong. The nurse gently approached my side and caressed my arm. "The baby will be fine. She just has pneumonia."

"Why did she say that?" I asked.

They all looked at my mom for an answer. She looked bewildered and shrugged her shoulders. "You never know."

The doctor looked at her like he had had a hard day and a long night. Then he told me my daughter would be taken to another hospital to receive better care. They brought her into my room in an incubator on wheels. She was so sweet. With my hand on her tiny glass world, I whispered to her and told her I loved her. The doctor and the transport team came to get her. They took a picture of her, gave it to me, and left. Four hours later, I escaped the hospital to be with my baby.

Augusta stayed in the ICU for two weeks. After she was released, we stayed between Trevor's mom's house and my parents' house. Life was beautiful and could not have been more perfect. Augusta brought us so much love and gave me a reason to live.

THE HORRIBLE EXPERIENCE IN THE desert four years earlier was now mostly a distant memory. An appropriate dose of anti-anxiety medication and antidepressants kept me stable. In public, I acted as normal as I could and mimicked other mothers. But at home, I practiced bizarre rituals daily.

One day, when Augusta was one year old, the police came to my parents' house and asked for me. The policeman told me I had to go to the police department immediately. He explained that I should not watch TV or listen to the radio.

My mom and I arrived at the police department forty-five minutes later. After I sat at a large executive table, I looked up to see the devil. The man who had tried to kill me four years prior was right in front of me.

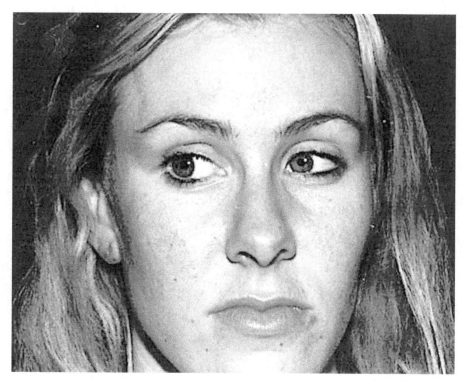

I was victim number five

CHAPTER TWENTY-TWO

Eight Girls

Acorns hit the top of my treehouse, and the wind gushes past as if motivated by fear. (Okay, they aren't really acorns; they are these little beige balls that look like garbanzo beans. They fall off the desert trees when the wind is rough. *Acorns* sounds more interesting.) With half a glass of cabernet left, I sip and stare at the words I type.

The *Double Dream* strain of marijuana is fitting for this evening. I smoke it out of a fragile object that in my mind resembles a crack pipe, though I've never seen one. This pipe is made of glass and is long and thin.

As I blow out the smoke, I watch it linger before my eyes. My hair is soggy, and my makeup is smeared because I recently swam in the pool. Tonight I write while naked. Sometimes, if I feel comfortable, I will do things like this. It's strange how vulnerability can give you a sense of power, and power is what I have.

With chemically-induced, squinted eyes, I feel alluring. The music is a perfect kind of loudness. "Something Just Like This" makes the treehouse rumble, as if The Chainsmokers and Coldplay are here in person on my deck. This song makes my soul feel safe and secure. Occasionally, music speaks to you. If you smoke a little pot and drink a bit of wine, it really speaks.

The twinkle lights hold my attention. The beauty captivates me. I want to stay in this moment, fully mesmerized by the parade of senses I experience.

But I begin to see a face. Its features are familiar—awful and unkind. As I acknowledge the man on the wall, I cock my head and sit up tall. *I am a fucking badass*, I think, nearly shouting it aloud. I crack a confident smile and zone in on the monster, as my treehouse reluctantly fades away.

Five photos are laid out before me while I cover my eyes with my hands. The detective instructed me to shut them, but I found that difficult to do. It would make me vulnerable to a threat. With my head down and my eyes behind my shaky hands, I imagined the devil's ugly face.

Since she wasn't told to shut her eyes, my mom viewed the photos first. She probably examined them and searched for a monster, but he does not look like a monster to anyone but me, so she would never guess correctly.

As I waited, I trembled. The detective spoke.

"When you open—*uncover*—your eyes, examine the photos and let me know if you see the man who kidnapped you."

The detective spoke with a voice that reassured me the man's photo *was* in the lineup.

Because I knew the picture was on the table, I did not want to move my hands away from my face. My fingers were all that separated my eyes from the evil face that had haunted me throughout the years.

After I was told to remove my hands, I decided to keep them on my face. This was my way of saying, "Nope. Sorry. The ball is in my court now." The rebellious thought gave me a sense of control. The next move I made would prove that my story had been true after all. So I tried to savor the moment and make others hang for once. *Why was everybody so interested in something that I had made up?* I thought, with sarcasm echoing through my mind. The detective was nice and probably didn't deserve my childish attitude.

"You can move your hands, Ms. Asbenson."

When I finally obeyed his request, I couldn't help but laugh at my peculiar behavior. Then I looked up at the face of the devil, and my smile vanished.

"That one," I said.

The sound of my voice was unfamiliar, so firm and sure. With complete assurance, I pushed the photo toward the detective.

"Look at the others, Ms. Asbenson."

"No need. That's him."

"Look at the—"

"I don't know them! This is him!" I said, after I gave the photos a quick glance and pulled the monster's face back in front of me.

"Okay," he said.

The expression on his face suggested there was something wrong. I was confused.

"What?" I asked.

He seemed reluctant to speak his next words.

"This guy was arrested in Chicago," he said as he tapped the photo and took a giant breath.

There were brief pauses between his next sentences as if he struggled to tell me the severity of what had happened. "He is a serial killer. He killed eight women. And you are the only one who got away."

There are times when I reflect on the moment I received verification of the horrors that had altered my mind and my life so fiercely. Those few minutes in the police station replay in my head, and I think: *Wow, that's freaking crazy! Why me? Why am I alive? What the fuck am I here for?*

My mind is blown. *I'm not perfect. I'm not the best out of all of these women. I'm no one. Why am I here? Why am I the only one out of all eight girls?* I take another puff off the "crack pipe" and look around the treehouse.

Smoke begins to cloud the air, and my eyes scan my surroundings. *What have I done?* I wonder. All of the news related to this case is plastered throughout my treehouse, covering the walls. The killer's ugly face stares from the covers of the newspapers.

My name stands out in every article, although it is not highlighted. Magazines read "The One That Got Away." There are pictures of me looking humbly determined. Sticky notes naming a slew of mental disorders have been posted about. My treehouse now resembles a detective's office, with a green glass legal lamp in the corner, like you see in the movies.

If the gardener stumbles upon my madness, what will he think? And the man in the house is going to assume I am nuts, if he ever comes in here. But does it matter if he thinks that? Maybe I am crazy. Perhaps it is okay if I am nuts, considering the experiences I have gone through.

Lost in the detective's words, an uncontrollable cocktail of emotions surged through my body. The various parts of my face contorted as my heart and mind felt the contrasts of terror and relief, sadness and triumph. My gut urged me to vomit as my mind encouraged me to celebrate.

My mom began to talk, and I wanted to put my hand over her mouth. This was my time, my redemption. My—whatever it was, it was mine.

"Can I talk to the girls, the other girls he hurt?" I asked, interrupting my mom.

The detective looked confused but remained gentle. "He killed all the other girls. You're the only one left."

My head felt heavy. Guilt filled my veins. The entire situation was bizarre.

The detective began to gather his notes. "We need to warn you that the news is all over this, Ms. Asbenson. They are going to call you and try to talk to you about this. They will want to interview you."

My confusion awkwardly turned to joy. *Is it appropriate to combine mourning with pride?* I wondered.

As we left the office, all eyes were on me. People saw greatness in me, a quality I had never seen in myself. A few people at the police department shook my hand and told me that they admired me. Their admiration seemed like nonsense, but I enjoyed every minute of it. For the first time in my life, I felt special and important, like a movie star.

I'm on the deck of the treehouse. The most comfortable spot, surprisingly, is on my back, sprawled across my queen-size air mattress. There is a tiny hole, and the mattress deflates with a faint whistling scream. The weather is ideal, and I notice a slight breeze. Newspapers wave up and down on the bamboo fence that has become the walls of my deck.

The treehouse now physically represents my past. When I enter, it brings me places I may or may not want to go. In order to tell my story, I must endure the discomfort that too often surfaces. The reminiscent decorations help propel me to the past. Instead of going directly back in time, I swirl around in the memories like I am on a merry-go-round.

After I roll onto my side, I stare at the face of the ugly human on a newspaper page. He stares back. I do not plan to look away. His death-like, pale face begins to produce color, and the hair on the sides of his head begins to blow away. He is now bald, and he wears black-rimmed eyeglasses. He is older, maybe in his fifties. His drab white T-shirt transforms into a suit and tie. He sits straight. Our eyes are still locked. I am not in the treehouse anymore …

It is the year 2018. The courtroom is filled with people. As my eyes engage with his, I refuse to look away. I want to smile at him because I know evil despises happiness. *Why is he staring at me? Is it strange that I am not afraid?* I ask myself. My lips seem to be moving. *Wait. Where am I again? Oh, my goodness. I am in court. Why do I feel detached from myself as I speak? Who are all of these people?*

Focus. Tell your story.

Am I crying? Everyone watches me. Their eyes are on my lips, their hearts dangle from my every word. Supporters are here for me, although they don't know me. The spectators know me from the newspapers, magazines, and TV shows. My parents are not here to support me, but they have an excellent reason not to come. As I speak, my mind roams about, and I begin to experience flashbacks. Maybe this is the PTSD joining me in this event.

My story has been told a thousand times. Sometimes, when I share the details of the kidnapping and escape, I think of other things. Now I think about how important I feel. The families of the murdered girls will receive justice, and I will see to it. The world will be a better place because I shared my story. If I help one person, I will have succeeded.

As I sit on the black swivel chair behind a wooden podium and tell my story, I remember everything the first detective said when Andrew Urdiales was initially captured. A whirlwind of thoughts takes over my mind, and I go back again—back to what happened after the man was captured.

Me in self-defense class

CHAPTER TWENTY-THREE

Lost and Found

When the man who tried to kill me was finally caught, my younger sister came to me and admitted to writing *I WAS HERE* on the bathroom window. She explained that the words had just been a prank. Because the police got involved, she decided to keep quiet when she realized the gravity of the situation. I chose to forgive her, even though that message on the window drove me to sleep on the roofs of houses and underneath beds for four years.

Like everyone else, my little sister was unaware of the seriousness of the situation, and I couldn't blame her for that. Apologies weren't forthcoming from the people who hadn't believed me, so I decided not to expect any. From an outsider's perspective, I seemed to have come out unscathed, which did anything but inspire such apologies.

After what I had been through, there was a huge possibility that the soul I so desperately sought out would fall through the cracks. But I did a good job hiding my injuries. So much so that my happiness and good health seemed to outshine those of others around me. While they walked, I skipped. While they talked, I sang.

To drastically change my outlook on life, I was keen on adopting a perspective that focused on the beautiful, placid side of everything. I also mustered courage to go in search of lost bodies.

My room was swamped with newspaper articles, flyers picked up from bulletin boards, and an old collection of missing persons' milk containers from the '80s. The cardboard containers were attached to some old Christmas lights hung over my daughter's crib, and the walls were covered with the haunting papers.

Sometimes, when I stared at the children's faces, I became overwhelmed by thoughts of who they were and who abducted them. It unsettled me when I thought of them suffering through the same ordeal I had experienced. These innocent children were too young and fragile to defend themselves or to escape.

As I watched my daughter sleep, I imagined how I would lose my mind and be institutionalized indefinitely if anyone ever hurt her. In the same vein, I shuddered when I thought of the fear that gripped the families of the lost children.

My new train of thought urged me to action. Unfortunately, it was likely the missing children had been murdered. Deep down in my heart, the feelings about that possibility were extremely intense. These overwhelming emotions drove me to go out on searches. From place to place, I drove around looking for the bodies of these angelic children.

Although I was quite nervous to stumble upon one of them, I persisted with a strong sense of obligation. A serial killer had nearly murdered me. So I became motivated by the fear I had felt when I imagined my body would be thrown into the desert like trash and possibly eaten by coyotes at nightfall.

My remains could have disappeared forever. But the hope that someone would have found me early enough and gently covered me up also crossed my mind. All of these thoughts rushed through my head because I had been so close to death's door.

As a spiritually conscious person, I know I would have been in heaven by the time someone found me, but I would still prefer to be found quickly. My body would hold clues and answers that could eventually help catch my killer and prevent future murders.

What really drove me to search for the children was the profound love I felt for them. They were precious and innocent, and they deserved to have someone look for them. My nature and will turned me into that someone. The search for the dead became one of my main reasons to live. When I searched for their bodies, I felt the divine spark light up in me. Because I felt a unique bond with these children, there was a strong drive in me to become their hero.

My new hobby seemed strange to some, but I didn't care what others said. That task and my daughter were the threads that held me together.

"Birds sing after a storm; why shouldn't people feel
as free to delight in whatever sunlight remains to them?"
–Rose Fitzgerald Kennedy

The blow-up bed in my treehouse has lost enough air that my body begins to sink into the middle. My heart is still, and I feel powerful. The photos of the man on the walls bring me joy. His ugliness reveals my beauty. It took me over twenty years to realize that love conquers hate. When I found love for myself, everything else fell into place. My fears vaporized, and I became courageous.

In order to release the emotional hold that he had on me, I forgave him. When I forgave him, he disappeared from my nightmares, and I gained power. He did not destroy me, and he never will. He is weak. I am strong.

When I faced him in court, I felt no fear. He did not know me, and I did not know him. He dragged me to hell once but would never have the ability to do that again. He was locked up behind bars and could not harm me. So I released his grip on my heart. The choice was and has always been mine, and when I realized this, my life changed.

While raising my daughter, I began to transform myself into the person I had always wanted to be. One of my greatest desires had always been to become a storyteller and to feel important. I was featured on TV shows, and everyone was interested in what I had to say. Of course, it felt bizarre that the story I was telling was so horrible.

Why couldn't this be a better story? Why couldn't I have a story that swept people off their feet? A story that, when on TV, didn't need to have a warning disclaimer? Why isn't my story a beautiful one of trial and triumph? Why do I feel like I have the plague after telling my story? These are the questions that often ran through my mind.

It seemed as if God had answered my prayers of being on TV and being a storyteller, and I assumed it was because He knew I would be a great witness for Him. From inside that dark trunk, I had promised God that I would tell everyone He helped me get out. My testimony was now broadcasted around the globe. If this was all I was meant to do, then why did my childhood involve such bizarre circumstances?

To be honest, I had always known that the kidnapping and my survival wasn't all there was to it. This story alone was not why I was here. There had always been this part of me that knew I had a much bigger story to tell. What I really needed to do was to convince myself to show the world the bigger picture.

Eventually, I started asking TV shows if I could mention other parts of my life during the interviews. Every time, they told me that no one was interested in my life story; they only wanted "the story of survival." My response was always that my life story was indeed a story of survival. Sometimes they let me talk because, well, I'd do it anyway. But when each show aired for public viewing, my excitement became short-lived when I found that the segment about "my life" had been edited out and left on the cutting room floor.

Deep down, I knew my entire story would one day be told. For many years, I waited for someone to ask me for it. No one ever did, but I still told everyone that my story would be made into a book and a movie. There was never a shadow of a doubt.

In the meantime, I worked toward making my story even better. My acting and storytelling skills landed me multiple roles in community plays. At a local college, I took classes to better myself. My co-curricular and extracurricular activities included reading, singing, theatre makeup, public speaking, kickboxing, running, radio and television announcing, and acting. In every class, I earned an A. And I changed a law regarding murder (special circumstances), fought to keep the death penalty in California, spoke at schools about safety, and took self-defense courses.

To be honest, I failed the running class. But that's okay. When my life depends on it, I know I can run fast, so I don't mind not being able to run at top speeds for sport.

OVER A PERIOD OF NEARLY twenty years, I worked at more than thirty different jobs. At some of the jobs, I got into trouble for having too much fun. In those situations, I went overboard with my tendencies of trying to make others happy.

Once, I was a substitute teacher, and I was reprimanded after I let the students play hide-and-seek when class was in session. An over-zealous child broke the toilet seat in the classroom's private bathroom.

At another job, I put a fake spider on the desk, and when a patient approached, I would squeeze the inflator at the end of a tube attached to it, and the spider would jump high into the air. Because it was a cardiology office and my trick could cause a patient to have a heart attack and die, I was not allowed to scare patients, my manager said.

A kind man brought grapefruits to another job. The idea to make fake breasts with the fruit suddenly jumped into my head, and I put two in my shirt and pretended they were my boobs as I checked in the patients. When I stood up, one fell out and busted on the floor. Needless to say, I was scolded.

While working at Target, I rode the carts around and pretended all the boxes I opened were Christmas gifts for me, not items to stock on shelves. It was all fun and excitement for me, until one day when they called for backup cashiers and I tried to hide. Terrified to work one-on-one with the public, I hid in the stockroom. The assistant manager found me and made me help check out the customers. When I stood at the register and stared at the keys, it all looked quite foreign. The faces of the people in line were also bewildering.

Their expressions were a mix of kind consideration and annoyance. They listened as I tried to explain that I had never worked a cash register before. And I know they believed me—until a male employee on another register overheard me and said I had. At that instance, I was left breathless and felt my throat tie up.

The thought that something terrible was about to happen grew stronger. My emotions, not my mental faculties, did the imagining. The feeling of apprehension was just so strong. My eyes turned red hot, and I looked around frantically for someplace to hide. I began to cry. Tears were everywhere. Then suddenly I had a jolt of energy. I struggled to mouth the word sorry to the perplexed customers, and then I ran straight out the door and down the road.

My jobs were always short and sometimes terrifying. For many years, my life as an adult was full of struggles.

To this day, I still face challenges. Diagnoses have shown that I have manic depression, a.k.a. bipolar 1. My case is the one with rapid cycles. It is technically called rapid cycling bipolar.

The episodes come frequently. When I am depressed, I am so depressed that I cannot physically sit up. And I cry until I am short of breath. My stomach inflates and deflates abruptly. My face turns red. My breathing becomes very shallow. The only thing that brings joy and relief is nothing other than leaning against the shower wall as I watch my tears drift into the water stream and swirl down the rusty circular drain. Sometimes I wonder how long it would take me to sit in that shower and cry all of my tears out.

The depression hits me out of the blue and can go on for days. It never occurs to me that a certain situation might have triggered an episode.

Other times, I'm thrilled. So manic, in fact, that I believe I can complete any task in the world that I want, that I can be who I want.

Sometimes I want to skip around and ride shopping carts, but I know it is not socially acceptable at my age. So I usually bite my nails instead while I ponder other fun activities to indulge in. Other times, the urge is so powerful that I give into the mania and ignore the invisible critiques.

The maniac mood forces me to bake, dance, sing, and even talk to animals. It is easy for me to find beauty, cuteness, and funniness in everything. When I am maniacal, I have so much optimism and energy.

Once, I imagined the view of the mountains from the backyard would look better if a clueless and colossal tree wasn't in the way. Without a second thought, I went to the store and purchased a chainsaw. As I munched on a dill pickle, I watched internet videos on how to use the weapon. Within minutes, I skipped in the backyard with goggles on and slayed the deformed beast.

When the tree was gone, I regretted cutting it down. Plus, I was worried I might get into trouble, not only because this was my boyfriend's house, but also because the tree fell into the neighbor's yard.

Sometimes I am manic when I write. When I am maniacal, my imagination soars. My writing is stronger and more creative—like right now. Right now, I am manic. But I'm also a bit sad. It saddens me to know that I need to complete this book soon, and that I'll lose my connection with you. Finishing the book is definitely a must, but I want to write on to keep our bond. The connection between us is so real to me that I feel like I know you and you know me. My imagination projects your face as you're looking at this book. It shows me you are sad too. But hold on. If you know me by now, you know I will not leave without a grandiose good-bye.

My daughter Augusta

Chapter Twenty-Four

There's No Escaping You

My treehouse stands calmly in the presence of a warm, gentle wind. The sun sets behind the picturesque mountain that was once obstructed by a thriving but disfigured tree.

I'm here, too—manic but happy. Today was a good day. The soundtrack of my life plays in the background. My time here is almost over, and the journey has been bittersweet. My mind can't decide whether to smile or cry, so I sit in limbo and ponder my departure.

The newspapers that covered the treehouse walls have been removed and replaced with tinsel curtains. The long, silver, shimmering streaks flow in the light breeze as my fall-scented candles reflect in their sheen. The beauty I've created here brightens my soul.

Since my pee bucket has endured foul situations, it only seemed fitting to shove all the scary newspapers in it. No image of the monster who tried to extinguish my flame remains here in my sanctuary.

I feel powerful and liberated. As I breathe deeply, I close my eyes and sit tall. A sigh of relief exits my breath. My emotions are a kaleidoscope of sadness and excitement, gain and loss. It's time to say good-bye. Prepare yourself …

I'm going to tell you the answers to the questions still
lingering in your head.
Who is alive and who is dead?

Ten years prior to the writing of this book, my mom passed away from ovarian cancer. Her demise began with words that fell on deaf ears as she complained about pain often. She told us she had pre-cancer. About a year after she initially introduced the diagnosis of her disease to the family, she died.

Before her death, I'm sad to say my mom and I never developed a perfect relationship. During her time in hospice, I did attempt to make amends with her by searching the town for her favorite tea—raspberry iced tea. It had to have the tiny, crushed ice, she said. When I delivered the tea to her nearly two hours later, she yelled at me because I took so long.

Even though my mom and I never saw eye to eye, I did notice her relentless desire to advocate for the disabled. Her hard work was admired over the years as she continued to support the rights of children and adults with disabilities. She put the *active* in *activist* and did things like catching a bus at two in the morning with other activists to go to Sacramento and "fight the fight."

The fight in Sacramento was a push to have handicap-accessible bathrooms put in every public facility in California. She had also worked on a class action lawsuit for children who received a "bad batch of baby shots" in the '70s.

My brother was one of those babies.

It is now believed that Jay Jay's seizures and other mental handicaps came from those shots. The paperwork she was given for the lawsuit was too much to complete in the allotted time, so she did not receive money.

My mom was never treated or diagnosed with mental illness.

The diagnoses I came up with inside my treehouse led me to feel compassion toward her. I do not agree with how she treated me as a child, but I am no longer being mistreated by her. I cannot allow myself to be an emotional hostage of someone who no longer exists. Although I do not miss my mom, I have forgiven her in my heart. I will forever love and miss "Alice."

A few years after my mom passed away, my dad fell ill. He developed celiac disease, and beer became off-limits. When he could no longer drink and my mom was no longer in the picture, my siblings and I began to develop a wonderful relationship with him.

A year after he was diagnosed with celiac disease, he was diagnosed with three different types of aggressive cancer. He could no longer work. My sisters and I would all visit him often, as he still cared for Jay Jay in the dome house he had built.

On one particular night, my dad was in significant pain. After I explained how marijuana could help, he smoked some of it for relief. Soon after, he saw a donut on a TV commercial. He made me rewind it eight times!

"Jennifer," he said in a minor daze. "Get me some Krispy Kreme Doughnuts."

"Dad, I can't get you those. You are celiac. You *will* die!"

"Krispy Kreme Doughnuts would be the best way to go."

"I will go to jail for assisted suicide!" I said. But he wouldn't hear it. So I left the house and found some in a convenience store. I struggled to buy them. The cashier probably thought I was nuts because I just stood there and stared at the doughnuts for a few minutes, as I imagined my dad's joy, then his demise. Surely, the doughnut display had never caused anyone to cry, ever.

Along with one ticket to prison, I purchased the doughnuts. Fortunately, one final scrap of self-preservation kicked in. To save both my dad and myself, I sat in the car and ate every single doughnut. Not bad as far as epic sacrifices go.

My dad ended up forgetting about the tasty gluten treats, so my fears of relationship death by doughnut were quickly eased.

Before my dad moved to heaven, we skydived together. To continue along with his thrill-filled sprint toward the finish line of life, he also drove a race car with my brother around a real racetrack. He told me it was "the most fun he ever had." I'm glad he had the pleasure of saving the best for last.

He began to say *I love you* every time we spoke, and I knew he did. He kept that up for years before he finally made his departure from this world.

My faith and imagination tell me that my dad is just fine. He is probably working on a greasy, white car with Grandpa, while my mom tells a story of a two-headed angel to Grandma Beulah as she boils up her famous potato dumplings.

"Do the best you can." This was my dad's advice to everyone, and he is the perfect example of a man who did the best he could. I forgive him and will love him always.

After my dad passed away, Aunt Janine invited all of us siblings and our children to my amazing Grandma's ninety-sixth birthday party in Florida. Of course, Jay Jay and his new caretaker were invited too.

My sisters and I rented a spectacular themed house to accommodate our entire family, including my daughter and the man in the house. It felt appropriate to include Tyler too, since she now traveled the United States in search of adventures in a motorhome with her tail-wagging dogs and enthusiastic boyfriend.

After we celebrated my grandma's birthday, Janine asked if she could talk to me in private about the book I'm writing. As the man in the house scrubbed the grill and Augusta tried to convince a terrified Jay Jay to get the pretend alligator out of the pool, Janine and I found a quiet spot to sit on the back porch.

"Since you are writing a book about Alice," she said, "I thought you should know the truth."

I nearly knocked my wine over to get closer to her. "The truth?"

"When Alice passed away, a few of your family members approached me to tell me that your mom didn't like me. Did she ever mention anything like that to you?"

I told my aunt about the snide comments my mom made about Janine while we were growing up. She was shocked. For all of those years, she had no idea.

Then another shocker came.

"Your mom confided in one of your aunts why she didn't like you."

My heart dropped. Obviously, I was nervous. But there was another feeling. It was as if a muscle somewhere in my body that had been tensed all my life was starting to loosen up. My lifelong search for this answer was about to conclude.

"Why?"

"Because you reminded her of me."

My jaw dropped as the flashbacks of my life began to make sense.

"Right before she passed away, she kept repeating one thing."

With my head tilted, my eyes implored her to continue.

"She said, 'I love you' over and over again."

I repeated the words as a question. "I love you?"

She nodded.

I leaned closer. "That means she loved me."

Aunt Janine smiled. "Yes, it does."

Finally, I had what I had wished for my entire life. But it no longer mattered; I already had learned to love myself.

After Janine and I spoke, the party's alcohol began to flow and the night took on a life of its own. Tyler and my sisters and I all ended up with our feet in the pool as we talked about old times.

"Whatever happened to our goats Dolly and Alphie?" I asked.

My sisters looked at each other with their eyebrows raised, then looked at me with concern. Janna took a sip of her beer.

"You don't know?" she asked.

"No! Wait. Know what?" I asked.

Instantly, the pool grew silent. Janna and Gina struggled to hold their laughter back.

"We ate them!" Gina said.

Tyler looked disgusted as she splashed us with water. "Gross!" she yelled.

Naturally, we all busted up with laughter until we lost our physical composure. Gina snorted as she attempted to keep her eyeglasses from falling into the pool. After I dried the tears from the laughter, I paused for a breath of air and then asked one final question.

"For real?"

In the stillness and solitude of my treehouse, an intense feeling wells up from within me. An emotion so powerful, no gift in the world could ever replace it, but it could replace all the gifts in the world. The emotion is self-love. As I stand, I realize my unique powers. The anthem of my life, courtesy of The Rolling Stones, begins to play— "She's a Rainbow."

The wind picks up, and the sticky notes of diagnoses start to blow around. After I grab them, I shove them into the toilet-bucket with the newspapers.

My mind is brilliant. My imagination not only protects me, it gives me life. Who cares if I'm different? At least I have an exciting life.

While I scan my surroundings, a newspaper pokes out of the bucket and catches my eye. For a second, I stare.

With a large black marker, I scribble the words to oblivion and shove the paper back down into the bucket. I skip away from the treehouse with a glass of wine in one hand and the bucket in the other. As I sit on a wobbly-legged lounge chair, I find a joint in my pants pocket and begin to smoke it.

Free from distraction, I take in the scene: the foreground and background, the twinkly-lit treehouse, my glass of wine, and the joint.

Untroubled, I toss the spliff into the bucket and gently drip my glass of wine on top. With the strike of my lighter, my collection turns to fire, and I watch it burn.

From the table near me, I snatch a newspaper. *ANDREW URDIALES HANGS HIMSELF TWENTY EIGHT DAYS AFTER BEING SENTENCED TO DEATH*, it reads. The paper is shoved into the flames.

As my brightened eyes watch the paper dissolve into ashes, a certain few words pique my interest. "Jennifer Asbenson is now writing a book called *The Girl in the Treehouse*." A smile frames my face. Who I am and who I've always been have been revealed to me.

All along, I knew my true story. Everyone who has ever harmed me in any way has been forgiven, and I have forgiven myself. No longer am I "The One That Got Away." I am, and always have been, "The Girl in the Treehouse."

Through the smoke of the flames, I travel toward the past,
just one last time.
Needless to say, you follow as
The Rolling Stones continue to play.

I tell myself daily that I am fearless

Me, going places

CHAPTER TWENTY-FIVE

My Mind

*D*usk. My beautiful treehouse—more of a cottage these days—is all grown up. The dwelling is so large that I can no longer see the tree that supports it.

Suddenly, reality fractures. From the rift comes a tornado of change, of time. Roots creak and strain as they rip away from the Earth's tight grasp. Boards on the treehouse tremble against the nails and screws that hold them in place. One by one, wildflowers, shrubs, and flowers are uprooted. I'm sprayed with clumps of dirt sent flying by the upheaval.

Most of the structure, even wood from the treehouse, pulls away and whips by, dangerously close to my face. Because I'm in control of the storm, I do not feel fear. Nails and hammers cut through the air to someplace far, far away. Bricks and rocks fly by. The lights, once strung beautifully across the pool, stream past my head, still lit. They leave glows and streaks of charged air in their wake. More graceful than violent, the grapevine on the walls and the window screen unwinds itself before it escapes into the air.

So many flowers are in the sky.

To my surprise, I see a potato emerge from its hiding place beneath the ground and take flight. The entire treehouse deck is now gone. There goes the wine bottles and their accomplices: the joints and pipes. Amid all the chaos and deconstruction, there is one resurrection. A felled tree turns upright again, reattaching itself to the stump that once made it whole. It lives again. And a chainsaw—the murder weapon—takes flight and tumbles through the air, away from the scene of the crime.

A plastic toilet seat makes its departure, followed closely by an unwinding roll of toilet paper. My bucket of smoky papers dumps out and flies away with the rest of the man-made toilet.

Colorful rugs, Christmas lights, and sticky notes catch the wind and go swirling into the sky. My music speakers rush past, playing a beautiful swan song of the hymns they use to breathe. A Bible flies by, followed closely by a calm within the storm. Time continues to move, clouds still swirl, but the remaining parts of the treehouse are afraid to let go. They're rattling, but holding in place.

The backyard is now bare, reverted to a time when the treehouse was just an ugly fort struggling to stand on four legs. A noise builds from around the corner. It sounds like an old creaking dock. Four pieces of waterlogged plywood fly into the yard and attach themselves around the bottom of the fort. The panels create a box. One of them has the rough shape of a door carved into it.

Paint chips fly through the air, coalescing from nowhere; they attach to the structure and take shape as graffiti. Stickers join the party, adhering to the wall. A nudie magazine flies by. Of all the flying items, that one makes my eyes go wide.

A rackety, rusty ladder comes tumbling forth, and then I hear cans. They sound like the calamity that traditionally follows close behind a "Just Married" sign. These are beer cans, though, and no one has been married. They fly by, some landing on the roof like monuments, others fall to the ground.

As with the nails, hammer, and chainsaw, I have nothing to fear when spiders fly by and nestle back into their cozy webs in the fort.

You can only see my face. I have been crying. The fresh bottle of wine I sip from tells you it must be a different day, but you are not sure. I stare at the run-down old fort that the man in the house built for his sons long ago. I look worn down; I feel it, too. In my eyes, you can see the new lens through which I view the world.

Inside my mind, there is another tornado. I cannot physically stay still; the mental winds are so strong. In my thoughts, I have always been able to imagine shacks into castles. With my two hands, I have been able to resurrect these powers from my mind into reality. Who knew I was about to fulfill my biggest dream of all?

There are crickets now. Not whipping through the air, but chirping placidly. They provide the score to a brief interlude as everything goes black.

Then there's an argument between a man and a woman. A door is slammed. Then silence.

THE NEXT MORNING, I WOKE with swollen eyes and an empty bottle of wine beside me. I also had the most horrible headache ever. Before I got out of bed, the man in the house knocked on my barricaded door. He proceeded to gently pry the door open and asked if I would like a cup of coffee.

"Yes, of course," I said.

Then I told him I was moving into the treehouse to write a book. "Treehouse?" he asked.

"With God, humor, and imagination, all things are possible."
–Jennifer Asbenson

P.S. To this day, I still don't know for sure if we really ate those dang goats or not.

About the Author

*J*ennifer Asbenson is a survivor in more ways than most people ever encounter in their entire lives. Despite the challenges Jennifer faced early on, she has learned to rely on her belief in God, her sense of humor, and her imagination to overcome all adversities.

As the only surviving victim of Chicago serial killer Andrew Urdiales, Jennifer knows firsthand the aftermath of living through a life-threatening experience. She continues to be an advocate for the victims who cannot speak for themselves and strives to speak on behalf of mental health awareness. She suffers from extreme PTSD, OCD, bipolar disorder, and debilitating anxiety. Through forgiveness and self-love, Jennifer has regained control of her life and has learned to accept and love herself as she is. When not journaling or helping advise PTSD survivors, Jennifer spends her time taking college courses and reading self-improvement books. She also loves to go on adventures with her support dog Wesley.

Jennifer has been featured on many media outlets including *I Survived, 48 Hours*, and *The Dr. Oz Show.*

Additional photos and promotional material can be found at:
www.thegirlinthetreehousebook.com

Thank you for buying and reading this book. If you enjoyed it, I would greatly appreciate your submitting a review to share your enthusiasm. Thank you.

If you or someone you know is struggling with PTSD or involved in an abusive situation, please use the following resources:

Suicide And Crisis

The **American Foundation for Suicide Prevention** provides referrals to support groups, mental health professionals, resources on loss and suicide prevention information. Phone: (888) 333-2377

The **National Domestic Violence Hotline** provides 24/7 crisis intervention, safety planning and information on domestic violence. Phone: (800) 799-7233

The **Suicide Prevention Lifeline** connects callers to trained crisis counselors 24/7. They also provide a chat function on their website. Phone: (800) 273-8255

Mental Health Conditions

The **Anxiety and Depression Association of America** (ADAA) provides information on prevention, treatment and symptoms of anxiety, depression and related conditions. Phone: (240) 485-1001

The **Children and Adults with Attention-Deficit/Hyperactivity Disorder** (CHADD) provides information and referrals on ADHD, including local support groups. Phone: (800) 233-4050

The **Depression and Bipolar Support Alliance** (DBSA) provides information on bipolar disorder and depression, offers in-person and online support groups and forums. Phone: (800) 826-3632

The **International OCD Foundation** provides information on OCD and treatment referrals. Phone: (617) 973-5801

The **Schizophrenia and Related Disorders Alliance of America** (SARDAA) maintains the Schizophrenia Anonymous programs, which are self-help groups and are now available as toll free teleconferences. Phone: (240) 423-9432

The **Sidran Institute** helps people understand, manage and treat trauma and dissociation; maintains a helpline for information and referrals. Phone: (410) 825-8888

TARA (Treatment and Research Advancements for Borderline Personality Disorder)offers a referral center for information, support, education and treatment options for BPD. Phone: (888) 482-7227